THE YEAR OF THE PUPPY

HOW A PUPPY BECOMES YOUR DOG

Alexandra Horowitz
Adapted by Catherine S. Frank

VIKING

VIKING

An imprint of Penguin Random House LLC, New York

First published in the United States of America by Viking,
an imprint of Penguin Random House LLC, 2024

Visit us online at PenguinRandomHouse.com.

Library of Congress Cataloging-in-Publication Data is available.

ISBN 9780593351307

1st Printing

Printed in the United States of America

LSCH

Design by Lucia Baez

Text set in Nietos

This is a work of nonfiction. Some names and identifying
details have been changed.

THE YEAR OF THE
PUPPY

HOW A PUPPY BECOMES YOUR DOG

PART 0

GESTATION

I peek in the rearview mirror and see her asleep in the back seat. She's outgrown the little donut-shaped dog bed she first used, and now she is more lying on it than in it: her head and shoulders are fully on my son Ogden's lap.

Everything is slowly changing with her. It's that she folds her ears back against her head as she greets me. It's her new, rabbit-legged sitting posture. It's that she will now jump fully onto my lap and then snuffle, piglike, for a kiss. She chases her tail. She digs into the shoebox of toys and takes everything out, batting a ball around and flipping the long-legged and spindly Grinch around her head, banging herself on her sides. She has a way with each of us in the morning: *Aroooo!* she calls when we enter the room where she's sleeping. She has a way with each of the dogs. She and the cat are working it out, licking each other in turns. It's that even as she outgrows her dog bed, she is fitting into the family.

I met her right after she was born.

Our family did not need a puppy. We are three humans, two dogs, and a cat; our days are rich with interactions, and our home is replete with animal fur. Sometimes, though, an idea grips me. It appears from thin air, as though I simply walked into it and breathed it in. And once I've taken it in, it circulates in my mind, gradually and then relentlessly breaking through the hum of my brain's background noise. This time, the idea was simple: *puppy*.

It's a popular idea, puppies. But as attracted as I am to puppies' guileless manner, to their clumsy gait, and to the bigness of their excitement to see a person or their alarm at a bird taking flight, I was not attracted to the idea of *living with one*. For one thing, there are plenty of puppies about. I need only walk out of our apartment in New York City to see puppies—to see people with puppies, the people blearily standing in attendance with an overlong leash, waiting for a puppy to remember to pee. For another, one of the satisfactions of adopting dogs from shelters, as our family has always done, is knowing we are taking home a dog who needs a home. Often, that dog is not a young puppy but a dog who has already lived some life. I did not want to be implicated in *making* a dog who would need a home.

So a new puppy was off the table—or so I thought. Our last adoption, eight years earlier, was of three-and-a-half-year-old Upton, already eighty pounds of hound, sincerity, and goofiness when we met him. He arrived at our home needing surgery for an injury long suffered and never addressed. And he arrived with a mysterious set of fears—of noises, of his shadow—and with, it seemed, no experience at all of the things that were to become the substance of his life with us: leashes, sidewalks, elevators; people wanting to pet him, dogs wanting to sniff him. We met him at a shelter to which he had been returned as a three-year-old (*Reason for return: have too many dogs*) after having been adopted from the same place as a puppy. Thus, included in the paper trail of his life that was delivered to us was a photo of baby Upton, all ears and smile.

I think that was when I first breathed in the idea. *Who was he as a puppy?* I wanted to know. The only sorrow of coming to know Upton was the great mystery of his life before us, of where those fears came from and of not being able to reach back in time and make it right. This sentiment is not uncommon. Few of us meet our dogs on day one. The dog who will eventually become an integral part of our family is born without us, into a family of their own. Their parents contribute genetically and, in the case of the mother, substantially after birth to what kind of dog this puppy will become. Their littermates, the world around them, the sounds and smells and sensations they are exposed to all will influence their personality. By eight weeks of age, they are developmentally equivalent to a year-old human baby—with all the walking, chattering, world-exploring milestones in their past—and they still won't be meeting their human family for weeks or months. When they first sniff the human visitors who pack them into the car at the breeder's or whisk them off from a shelter and bring them home, they are already partly who they will be.

Years went by, and the puppy idea was displaced by louder and more urgent ideas. But it bubbled up again as our dogs passed their eleventh and twelfth birthdays, officially well into the geriatric, or senior, stage in veterinary terms. We could not avoid the inevitable ending of their lives, but we might let them influence the next dog we would get to know. Who better to teach a new dog about the world—about *our* world—than our crazy, wonderful dogs? My son and husband made approving noises when I let the idea float out of my mouth and into the room.

I have no dearth of dogs in my life. Not only do I live in a city bursting with dogs, but I live with two already. In addition to Upton, our family includes Finnegan, a charming and endearing mutt who has endured the introduction of a child, another dog, and a cat with only the rare dagger-filled glare at us for so ruining his life. And I am a scientist of dogs: I study their behavior to try to understand their minds. I founded and run the Dog Cognition Lab at Barnard College, where researchers and I observe dogs who come onto campus with their people to participate in our experiments or who submit to our gaze at their homes or in the parks. As a scientist and author, I have surely typed the word *dog* tens of thousands of times. It finally occurred to me that I might bring a scientific eye to puppy development. As a bonus, I'd get to live with a puppy.

I had trepidations. Committing to taking on a lifetime of responsibility for another creature is no casual matter. Moreover, I was hesitant about a puppy's unrestrained enthusiasm disrupting the dynamic between us and our current dogs. At the same time, though, I wanted in on this mystery: if I couldn't know my own dogs as puppies, perhaps I could at least know this puppy into doghood.

The mysteriousness of this period of dogs' lives is accidental—an artifact of our society's way of thinking about dogs. Two hundred years ago, we had a different relationship with dogs. They were rarely living inside people's homes: more likely on the farm or on the street or underfoot than in our beds. The business of pure-breeding dogs had not developed and neither had the idea of a young puppy as something to be bought at a store with accessories to match. Unchecked breeding had not yet led to severe overpopulation, necessitating the development of dog pounds, then shelters and rescue groups, which usually negotiated the rehoming of a dog whose puppy days were waning or past. Two hundred years ago, people knew puppies. They witnessed births. The life course of animals, from beginning to end, was woven into humans' lives (not always to the animals' advantage).

No longer. And a secondary result of how we live with dogs now is that most people miss not only the birth and first weeks of life of their puppy but also effectively miss the first months of their puppy's life with them. The quick development of the dog—from underdeveloped newborn to overdeveloped teenager in a year—happens while their person is simply trying to both acclimate the dog and be acclimated to them. We get caught up in the house-training, walk training, bite training, don't-chew-everything training that is the typical contemporary approach to a dog's first months of life with a new family. In focusing on training a dog to behave, though, we mostly miss the radical development of puppies into *themselves*—through the equivalents of infancy, childhood, young adolescence, and teenagerhood—until it's already happened.

Most books about puppies are instructional: *Here's a compli-cated, furry, adorable piece of machinery you just carried into your home; how do you get it to run?* Instead of following an instruction manual for a puppy, I wanted to follow the puppy through intro-ductions to a new world—meeting suspicious older dogs, a playful feline with long claws, and an adolescent boy who, in his enthu-siasm and energy, bridges the world between dog and human. By slowing down to observe the changes in our new charge from week to week, I hoped to make new sense of the dog's behavior in a way that is missed in a focus only on training. I wanted to keep a lens firmly on the puppy's point of view—how they begin to see and smell the world, make meaning of it, and become themselves. And at each moment and developmental stage, I stepped back to consider what the science or history of dogs tells us that can shed light on the behavior of puppies. I wanted to compare our puppy's early days to those of wolf pups and to compare her development to that of another group of pups being raised among people but with the aim of becoming working dogs: professional detection dogs. In other words, this puppy was to be my subject and my dog, her actions experienced, scrutinized, and contextualized. Should we all get through it, I hoped to know her as I have never known a dog before.

I became a witness to the transformation of a mewling splodge of fur into an exquisitely sensitive, preternaturally agile, sweet, lov-ing creature. Into a member of our family. She is here with me now; come meet her.

PART I

A PUP IS BORN

JANUARY ❧ WEEK 0
Dear God, That's a Lot of Puppies

Time is moving in an irregular, disconcerting way now that we no longer have the usual cadence of leaving the house every day. During the pandemic, whether it's Friday or Monday hardly matters. But time passes anyway, and it's noticeable in both the season and the puppy. Against the sameness of our days, she is different every day, sometimes even from morning to night. I could measure time by her ears, which have been inching ever up, and then, one morning, dropped under their own weight, becoming floppy triangles again. I could track time in the speed of her behavior changes. First she comes when we call her; then she doesn't come. She learns to sit in a place; she learns to sit right near but not on the place. She stays on the first floor; then she learns about stairs; then she learns of the fun of running up and down stairs. She learns about squirrels, she learns about trees, she learns about squirrels in trees. She loves the water; she retreats from the water. The only thing that doesn't change is that every single day she seems surprised about the cat.

January 2020, the young dog was surrendered to a shelter when her owners realized she was pregnant. *Surrendered*, as in given up, handed over, abandoned. The dog herself has not given up. She wears the expression that many pregnant dogs seem to—of vigilance. Her amber eyes follow the motion of people nearby, while she keeps her back against a wall. Catching a glimpse of her head-on, I note the blaze of white between her eyes, the mottled merle coat, the ears that aim up but fall down. She is winsome, her bearing stolid. In profile her belly is swollen downward, making her legs look unnaturally short. Inside is an unknown number of pups, visible on X-ray as a cacophony of snaky vertebrae overlapping one another and round nuggets of skulls. She was probably due several days ago, Amy suggested, but held out while being transported from Georgia. Amy is her foster mom, one of the many miraculous folks who agree to house dogs in transition, going from homeless to homed, from scared to sociable. She is tall, dressed practically, with a shy smile. Amy has named the dog Maize. Not only has Amy agreed to take in Maize, she's taking in an indeterminate number of Maize's puppies, committed to raising them all to be dogs who will not be surrendered to a shelter.

Maize arrived in the middle of a rainstormy night, having been driven up the Hudson Valley, in New York, working against her body's drive to birth her pups. From the car she was walked in the rain to the house, where, though it was full of the smells and sounds of several other dogs and birds, she finally found a warm, dry spot and collapsed, relaxing into sleep.

The next morning, Amy was due at work early, so she left Maize in a comfortable setup with plenty of room to move around, soft spots to lie, water to drink. We cannot know, but it is likely that even with her stress at being in a new place, with new faces, canid and human, the sensations of her body began to take prominence, and she paced, panting and restless, finding no place to quell the tremors of muscular contractions beginning to ripple through her. She might have felt at once hot and cold, and as her cervix began to dilate, she worked to find a place to nest, digging into one surface after another until she finally settled.

What we do know is that when Amy returned several hours later, she found Maize settled on a soft bed placed in a plastic kiddie pool, her body curled around six small furry forms. Strictly speaking, of course, people don't need to be present for the birth of a litter. Most dogs are born without human assistance. Of course, dogs also get ill in delivery, bleed to death, or fail to aid their puppies after birth. When people are present, they are there to help in case of one of these emergencies and to be a redundant mother, in a sense. Watching a dog deal with a handful of puppies suddenly appearing from her bum, it is hard not to wonder how she does it. But she does, whether we assist or not.

Six puppies—still just suggestions of dogs, with all the parts but not yet themselves, their fur sleek with the remnants of the amniotic sac that was Saran Wrapped to them, keeping them alive in utero. Amy settles down outside the pool, talking admiringly to the mother, and lifts up one after the other, each one fitting comfortably in her hand, legs dangling, toes sprawled, as her hand envelops the belly. She towels each one in turn and replaces them by their mother, setting them near her belly, encouraging their mouths to a nipple with her finger. Everyone dried and at a spigot, she leaves the room to gather more supplies. When she returns, another pup has joined the six. An hour later she steps out again and returns to an eighth puppy.

Then she stays put. Maize is panting, looking entreatingly at Amy, at the space in front of her, and then suddenly lifts her top rear leg high up and ducks underneath it, licking her nether regions. There is a head there, thoroughly wet from the rupture of the amniotic sac, the nose bright pink. A front leg appears, and then another, all attended to by the tongue of the new mother, relentlessly licking each part. With each lick, the form is paradoxically less wet, as the remains of the sac around it are removed and its very short fresh hair is smoothed back by the mother's tongue. The pup, a boy, is motionless, except as the tongue jostles him and as he is expelled in spurts from the warm safety of mother's womb. With most of him out, she grabs more forcefully and pulls at him with her teeth—she has gotten hold of the umbilical cord and placenta, the organ of fetal-puppy life providing oxygen and nourishment that has just this second expired its usefulness. She drags it—and the puppy—over in front of her, gently pins him to the ground, and pulls off the whole thing, consuming it. The huddle of puppies along her flank mew plaintive sounds: *errm*s and *uumph*s and tiny screams.

The newest puppy has started to squirm. He is being jostled and pushed, and there is a strong pulling at his belly. Lying on his back, he does his first recognizable dog act, stretching his hind legs out long and pawing the air with his front legs. I can see each tiny finger of his paw: a miniature webbed hand drawn by a child, raised up in a herky-jerky wave to the world. Mom is back at her own bum, cleaning up, and the pup rests between her front legs. When the tongue stops its attentions, he lies there, stunned, the muscles of his face working to operate each of its early tools—the eyes (which will not open for weeks), the nose (which will soon lead him to a meal), the ears (the canals closed, with the outer ear flaps pressed back against his head), and the eyebrows (furrowed as though in deep concentration).

His tiny heart—running the length of just five tiny vertebrae—beats strongly, up to 220 beats a minute, each beat visible through his skin. His breaths come irregularly, faster than one a second as the lungs take the first of their great bellows blows of life, then slowing to one every few seconds. He is otherwise still, exhausted from his launch into the world. His mother's nose nudges him to movement. With her tongue she tumbles him around, and only when she relents for a moment does he curl his nails into the soft ground and get enough traction to pivot his body to almost turn over to his belly. Now he is working his limbs, swimming through this new water. Three minutes from the sudden expulsion from his home, he is breathing, moving, and making his way to rejoin his siblings on the other side of the belly they just left. The next pup appears rump-first, the tiniest of tails a quotation mark on this announcement. Maize ducks her head under her foot and is licking, and suddenly the pup is plunged out in a rush of bodily fluids, rolled into her siblings by the long persistent licks from her mother, who is alternating between cleaning herself up and licking madly around the new pup's tiny face. Somehow the pup gets free, grips the ground, army crawls right under an older sibling, and beelines as best she can toward mom's belly. Another appears, headfirst—especially noticeable as the head is completely green (probably meconium—waste matter—which can contain the bright green pigment biliverdin, making for a harmless but shocking hair color). Soon the puppy opens her tiny mouth and gives an early-morning stretch, even as she is still attached to her mom.

Maize keeps at it, her eyes wide. When not tending to a pup, she rests her head on the lot of them, her eyes darting around her.

By midnight there are eleven puppies sharing a birthday, five boys and six girls. *Whelp* is the very specific word used for female dogs giving birth—and that is just about the sound that I make as the final puppy appears. "Dear God," Amy says, sitting back, "that's a lot of puppies." The oldest, several hours into their lives, seem impossibly mature compared to the new ones: their bodies are dry, their fur plumped, and they are all directed toward their momma's belly, rumps mooning the world. The newest are scraggly and still moist, their bodies looking more fragile, just put together. They are on their backs, straining with the effort of just turning over.

There are three fewer nipples than there are puppies. The pups who can right themselves aim for a nipple, scrabbling over one another, and, finding it occupied, just take a nap. The end result is a towering puppy pile, making it hard to tell where one ends and another begins, despite their different colorations becoming more visible as their fur dries.

When any one of them falls off the pile, they lift their head, jerkily searching the air for wherever their warmth and comfort and food have gone. Pup legs are always gently pedaling, trying to pull them forward, closer, into. When Maize next rises, the puppies stay where they are. Their limbs splay, and their heads rest heavily on the ground. They look completely spent.

As I watch Maize manage one pup after another, I find that I am holding my breath. I am in awe—not just of the matter-of-factness with which she handles this turn of events and her impressive skill at it. I am watching life generate life. To see a new being go from *not born* to *born* feels as big as if I were witnessing that puppy's whole life.

A tired mother with her puppies

Maize raises her head, panting, looking momentarily stunned, and then goes back to tending her new charges. I finally take a breath, and something in me turns. Our new family member is in that pile.

8-8

Dog litters are five puppies strong, on average—more in free-ranging dogs, for whom the pup survival rate is lower, and fewer in smaller-size breeds. The largest litter recorded, by those who record such things, was a litter of twenty-four, to a Neapolitan mastiff. Producing such a gaggle might have taken that mother more than a day in labor, as the interval between births can be up to or beyond an hour.

Pups are birthed alternately from either side of the Y-shaped uterus. Where they are situated in utero affects their sexual development: right before birth, fetuses are exposed to a surge of hormones, especially testosterone and other androgens, which can tend a puppy toward maleness. Pups of many species who are at the far end of each uterine horn get the most nutrient-rich blood and are likely to have a higher birth weight. The fetuses are also affected by what their mom has eaten. If an unusual flavor is added to her diet, it passes into the amniotic fluid. The newborns then prefer water or milk with that flavor added over the unflavored version. So are they affected by their mom's travails. Stress during pregnancy can lead to more reactivity—essentially, overreaction to stimuli—in the puppies. In the uterus, and at birth, the different head shapes that so distinguish various breeds—the long face of the greyhound, the short face of the bulldog—have not developed yet. Everyone looks more or less like a wee pug.

Birth stimulates reflexes that the new mother likely did not know she had. She will eat the placenta and amniotic sac, which not only clears the newborn's airway but also is thought to avoid attracting predators that could be drawn by the odor. Eating the placenta also appears to alter the mother's hormone levels in such a way that her milk production is increased. The fluid from the amniotic sac functions as a prompt for the mother not just to lick but to begin to accept and bond with these strange forms that have just appeared. When researchers remove the pups straightaway, returning them after washing them, their mothers fail to interact with the pups, or reject them outright. The licking also prods a newborn puppy into action, and the mother's saliva kills off bacteria that could be fatal to the newborn.

Just as human babies born in hospitals have their vitals and reflexes tested within a minute of their entering the world, so do puppies. Are their gums a healthy pink, or blue? Is their heart rate the speedy 220 beats a minute or slower than 180? If a paw is pressed, do they whimper and move it? Flex their limbs and move their heads? Do they cry? Crying is, perhaps paradoxically for those who have lived with a newborn, always good: it is the proper reaction of a nervous system to the new, startling experience of being cold, hungry, and outside the womb. Absence of crying is a warning sign. Is their weight in the normal range? Pup size varies by breed, from a single ounce (Chihuahua) to over two pounds (Newfoundland), but averages six tiny ounces. More important than approximating the average weight at birth, though, is whether they gain weight in the next week.

For that, the pups have some responsibility. They need to muster their early reflexes and capacities to make it to mom's belly, and fast. By kneading their front legs against the warm, soft mom they have found, they help to encourage the flow of milk. They will soon each be drinking about five ounces a day, which is slightly less than the amount in many juice boxes. The kneading-suckling rhythm seems to stimulate a reward center in the mother. Researchers studying other animals (lab rats) have found that, for moms, the pups are themselves the reward. So mom is inclined to stay put—good for both mom and pups.

FEBRUARY ✿ WEEK 1
Sweet Potatoes

I pull into the driveway of Amy's home on a cold day. The sky is the kind of fathomless gray that makes you forget it could ever be blue.

I have come to see the puppies. As I knock, a commotion erupts inside—a chorus of barks, mixed with the sounds of dogs running and scratching the door. A dog nose appears suddenly from behind a curtain, then just as quickly retreats. As the door opens, more dogs dart out: kelpies, wagging and barking and jumping up. Two older border collies saunter among them, calm schooners surrounded by crazed motorboats. There are eight dogs here, plus two more, I learn, that Amy is fostering, in another room. And then, too, the puppies.

Amy lets me in, and we step gently through the carpet of dogs. A radio is playing, an appliance hums; the smell of a birch fire greets me. One wall of the room is lined with shelves of trophies and ribbons from dog-competition events: agility, sheepherding, disc, mushing. Another wall has a giant cage in which a cockatoo who is missing her back feathers side-eyes me warily. "I'm bird sitting," Amy explains, "and the people haven't come back." She gestures to another room, which has been given over completely to her own two parrots. At the same time, a calico cat saunters in and checks me out before sitting down to clean herself. Boxes of food and supplies donated for the fostered pups tower to the ceiling.

The new mom, Maize, is just visible outside the back of the house, staring intently at the screen door. I follow her gaze inside to the kitchen. I approach and navigate a baby gate, then climb over a makeshift wall segregating the kitchen appliances. Beyond that wall is a smaller pen, and within the pen is a small dog bed, and on one-half of the bed is a pile of eleven puppies curled around one another. That pile is the object of Maize's gaze.

Amy opens the door, and Maize runs in. Spotting a new person, she crouches submissively, and I also crouch and turn away to calm her. Amy places a large sausage of dog food on a plate for her, and she is calmed. We step into the pen and settle beside the dog bed. The pups, only several days old, are not quite dog-shaped yet; instead, they're lumpish forms the eye registers as living but whose species one cannot quite place. They appear to be perfect sweet potatoes with ears, feet, and a tail. A white sweet potato adjusts herself and morphs into a piglet, short of snout and pink of body.

We scoot the bed onto a heating pad. The pile shifts. It is just above freezing outside, and the puppies will not be able to maintain their own body temperature until they are four weeks old. They lack the necessary extra fat for insulation, and they cannot shiver to warm themselves. Each pup's body temperature is still several degrees below where it needs to be, and they instinctively keep one another's close company. In the pile they form, they can get close to the 101.5-degree temperature that's normal for adult dogs.

When Maize finishes eating she steps into the pen. Her smell steps in with her, the odor of milk and mom wafting over the pups. They stir as a heap, gently pulsing in her direction. Maize pokes her nose among the pups, licking and rousing them. She suffers my presence there with grace and even, guardedly, lets me pet her. Tiny heads lift, and mouths open, aimed mom-ward. At this age the puppies spend their lives mostly sleeping or nursing, and over the three hours that I am there, they do both, sometimes at once. The pups make soft squeaking, whimpering noises, shimmying over one another in the general direction of their mother's belly. As they make their way over to Maize, she licks each one's behind clean without comment. "She's a good mom," Amy says: patient, deliberate, and rump-cleaning.

When they fall off her belly, they collapse into the pancake-like posture typical of animals who cannot yet lift their heads for any length of time. After birth and their first meal, they each weighed between just eight and thirteen ounces. Eight ounces is scanty: a simple cup of coffee. (Coincidentally, I have seen many a wee pup weighed by being put *in* a coffee cup set on a kitchen scale—a sight that is off-the-charts adorable.) Now, only a few days into life, some have doubled their weight, while others are struggling. The tiniest pup, whom Amy has named Chaya, with a head smaller than my fist, is half the size of Pawpaw, a merle puppy—

his coat marked with patches of black, white, the gray called *blue*, and a copper called *red*, with moody dark makeup under each eye. I grasp Pawpaw and lift him toward me. He is heavy in my hand, but I can nearly circle his body when I close my fingers. Pawpaw squirms and utters a small gurgle, his paws outstretched, every toe reaching for ground. Each plump pad is an almost fluorescent pink, completely new out of the box. I set him down and grasp Chaya, then settle her between her siblings, where she has a chance at breakfast. A tan puppy with expressive eyebrows and a blaze of white, Pumpkin, coos at me, and I coo back to him as I stroke his soft back.

I gaze at them with astonishment. I feel let in on a secret, as a witness of this time in the lives of puppies. For now, it is not clear who is who; it is not clear that there is any *who* in there at all yet. In these early days of their puppyhood, eager to know them, we gather facts about their size and weight, comment on their colors, study whose ear is starting to stand upright. Later, when they begin showing distinct behaviors, we will note them all, collecting them like baseball cards—as though with each new fact or description, their true essence will be revealed to us.

We prod softly at the bodies to try to identify them all. Amy has named them for indigenous North American foods. Here are Fiddlehead, a blue merle with extra black markings, and three other merles, Calais Flint Corn (Flint), Blue Camas, and Persimmons, each with a distinguishing spot or fetching stripe of color. Underneath them we reveal Cholla Cactus, Acorn, and

Cranberry, whose colors vary from gold to white as a sunbeam enters a high window and moves across their backs.

The final pup is not among the pile at Maize's belly. Wild Ramps is a tricolor merle but mostly black, with a snout dipped in a white paint can and gold eyebrows. She is marooned on the puppy bed, the last one to whom it occurred either that *Oh, the smell of mom is near* or *Oh, the warmth of siblings is missing*, directing them toward mom. Her eyes, like those of all her siblings, are sealed closed in quiet protest at this bright world. Her ears, like those of all her siblings, are sealed closed in bright protest at this noisy world. She scooches herself on her belly, using the tools she has, pursuing warmth or smell, until she reaches the rim of the bed. Heading over the great wall, she topples dramatically, somersaulting and whimpering. Maize turns at her cries and licks her entire body in one long swipe, sending Wild Ramps onto her back. Righting herself, she heads straight for my knee, clothed in soft corduroy, and tests it for milk. I feel her tiny mouth puckered against it and am vividly aware of the inadequacy of my knee's offerings. I pivot her lightly toward the rump of another puppy. Then she need only climb him, creep up the length of his body, and at last nuzzle her way in to the desired belly.

☙

Puppies have a scant few months to figure out how to see, eat, communicate, move, deal with others, and find their way. This learning process starts in the womb, influenced by choices their mother makes. Once born, they need to make sense of not only other dogs but a whole nother species, *Homo sapiens*—enormously different from them in anatomy and behavior.

It starts small. To puppies at this age, the world is made up of the smells and the warmth of their mother and of one another. That's roughly it. They neither see nor hear. They cannot understand hands appearing from nowhere to lift them mom-ward, the sounds of our voices above their heads. They can do almost nothing: lifting their giant wobbling heads is a great effort; their wriggly crawling barely qualifies as forward movement. They cannot stand up. They can't lift a paw or wag a tail. They cannot roll on their backs. None of the small dog gestures so familiar to people who live with dogs is yet in their repertoires: they can't lick their tiny felted jowls, perk their ears, raise an eyebrow, lick a paw, or even pant. They do not sniff or blink. They can't stretch out; they can only knead their forelegs toward a nipple or smell of milk. They don't bark, growl, yodel, or howl. They can't pee or poo on their own; when they find themselves cold, a plaintive whine spills from them, directed at the great beyond. Their mother's role is to do for them what they cannot do for themselves and to keep them safe within their tiny worlds. As if to demonstrate, Maize grabs a wayward pup fully in her mouth and drops him by her belly; her licking prompts him to urinate and poo, and she cleans him up once he does.

They're in their neonatal stage, the period of about twelve days postbirth when, their capacities limited, their reflexes are tuned to keep them close to mom. But even in this blob-like state, when they are less *dogs* than *furry lima beans*, the puppies are having experiences. If they find themselves far from the smell of milk or the warmth of their siblings, their yelps broadcast their discomfort. Their motor skills are few. Though they can nurse enthusiastically, they are just lifting their heads when three days old and not even standing upright for another week. They have modest preferences. They creep toward warmth and away from a chill; sensible creatures, they will choose sleeping on cloth over sleeping on a wire surface. They find some smells disgusting (anise oil, quinine) and others lovely (milk). Some, it is instantly clear, have terrific nipple-locating skills: these are the pups who, over the first five days, double their body weight. We find others regularly stuck under one of mom's legs or fast asleep upside down, facing away from the belly while all their siblings nurse on it greedily.

For the first seven days of life especially, the puppies' brains are still getting organized. By putting tiny nets with small electrodes on their furry heads, researchers determined that the electrical activity in neonatal brains is about the same when waking and sleeping. The connections between the more ancient, subcortical areas of the brain and the cortex, where much of experience happens, are still being formed. Their sleep is active, visible in twitchy, dreamy kicks and shudders, and their waking time is sleepy. Studies on human infants have found that growth hormone is secreted in bursts in slow-wave sleep—deep sleep—so frequent deep, long sleep sessions lead to growth spurts. So, too, with puppies. Especially in that first week, a daily weight tally is informative about their health: a sudden decline in weight in the first two days is linked to a risk of early death. The best science suggests that puppies of all breeds should double their birth weight by the time they are a week into life. It is no surprise, then, that neonatal pups spend the majority of their lives asleep. Even so, they are definitely doing things—eating, scooting, yawning, rooting, stretching, reaching—and with that, they are learning things. At just a few days old, they learn to like the smell of their mom—or anything that's been near her.

In these early moments, they are already gaining knowledge about the great unfurry animals who will be in their lives: people. Puppies who are gently handled for just a few minutes a day from soon after birth grow up to be less reactive and fearful than puppies who are not gentled. In the 1960s and 1970s, the US military developed the Super Dog Program, which specified daily neurological exercises for young pups, in the hope of making them more successful working dogs. From the third to the sixteenth day of their lives, the puppies were run through five handled poses for three to five seconds apiece, each one intended to stimulate them in ways outside what their mom could provide. In one, a person holds the puppy head up, legs dangling, and tickles their toes gently; in another, the pup is carefully sent into a headfirst skydiving position, firmly gripped with both hands. Those super puppies who went through the program turned out to later have stronger heartbeats, improved cardiovascular functioning, more tolerance to stress, and greater resistance to disease than unhandled pups.

Since that program, a not-small amount of research has looked more carefully at the effects of early handling of newborn animals. Brave researchers have handled puppies for science: massaging their bodies; palpating their ears and muzzle; kneading their back, tail, and toes; and then flipping them over to belly-rub them. Surely this was arduous work. At eight weeks of age, these manhandled pups were slower to vocalize when alarmed, explored a new space more, and were calmer when left alone. Knowing this, I take care to scoop up each puppy in turn, running two fingers down their spine and lightly squeezing their delicate mouse paws, each digit a plump noodle finished with the tiniest and sharpest of claws. For the briefest moment, I set them on their backs in my open palms, their tails jutting just past my wrists. Each of the pups squirms a bit, stretching their toes to try to reach safe ground; one hiccups, and another sticks the tiniest tongue out at me.

These manipulations of the puppies are perceived by their nervous systems as small challenges—and while small, they appear to make the pups better prepared for the inevitable challenges of life. The kind of maternal care pups receive will influence their response to stress—an influence that will last their lives. The puppy's mother does her own sort of handling—licking, sniffing, nose poking. Those pups who receive higher levels of maternal contact become more exploratory pups later. Every dog will be confronted with the need to adapt to an uncontrollable world, to live with a different species; some will encounter the challenges of specific working roles.

Already we can see gestures that will evolve into familiar dog behaviors—into features woven into their personalities. Bunting—gently headbutting their mother, trying to find their breakfast—appears later as a sweet greeting of another dog or person. Your dog's nose bump of your leg as you're playing a video game is a leftover of their demands to their original parent. Similarly, early whines and cries aimed at getting mom to find them and carry them back to her eventually become the similarly high-pitched "alone" barks that come out of dogs left by themselves in your home: pleas for safety and companionship. They are becoming who they will be.

A puppy's life is structured around a few survival-related behaviors; similarly, a small set of reflexes organizes pretty much everything that a human baby does. Every parent who has wiggled each of their newborn's fingers or toes is essentially doing the baby equivalent of the handling tasks that benefit young dogs, too. The newborn brain is hurrying to get things in place, and in its rush, it mixes up wiring. But for pups, this will change in a blink.

FEBRUARY ❀ WEEK 2
Young Blue Eyes

Just one week and about seventy of their milk meals later, I see the puppies again. They form a great pile on a far corner of the dog bed, collapsed on each other willy-nilly as though a puppy pyramid suddenly fell asleep. One pup—the top of the ill-fated pyramid, presumably—is completely upside down, her nose poking out between a line of stout rumps. Even en masse, they are clearly changed from last week. Now they look like a heap of honest-to-goodness guinea pigs. Well, guinea pigs of mixed zoological heritage. They have tiny pink noses, more feline than canine; their heads are rounded and foreheads broad. The small noses of some of the pups are peppered with dark splashes; their white whiskers, grown out a centimeter in a week, sport a hint of black dye. The largest puppies dwarf the smaller. I gravitate immediately to the tiniest, Chaya, a tawny piglet lying off pile, and place her on the others. Her breath is malted milk and hay.

Within several minutes I have called them by five separate nicknames: little squibs, blobs, nuggets, puddle pups. Fuzz balls. They stir to none of those names. I gaze at the sleeping pile of fuzz balls. It heaves slowly with their breathing. Though I know each puppy is becoming themself, for now they are a group self. They have spent two months in a uterus packed tightly and now are just beginning to unpack themselves. Even at first glance, the puppies are clearly plumper and their bodies longer—gently taking up their space in the world.

When I look closely, I can glimpse small individual changes. This one's head is rounder; that one's brow is long and flat. They have expressions. Persimmons is calm, her face unperturbed; Flint rests with a slight gape of his mouth, as though continually amazed; the eyebrows on Pumpkin read worry. The scale tells us that almost all of them have doubled their birth weight, and now the heaviest is twenty-eight ounces, the lightest only fourteen.

It takes a few minutes before I notice the real change of the week. Maize rises, glances at me with full amber eyes, and pokes her nose into the pile. At her touch, the pile begins to stir, squeaking and grunting. And then I notice it. To see the slits of a puppy's eyes suddenly open is to see them transform: one minute they are fetal, and the next they are vividly puppy.

Newborn dogs' eyes usually open around two weeks, so at ten days these pups are a little precocious. Amy suggests that if, as she suspects, Maize actually held off birthing until she was settled, the pups might have been ready to be born a few days earlier. To be sure, not everyone's eyes are fully open. Amy lifts up one of the tawny pups, Pumpkin, to take a closer look. He has only one eye sleepily open: the left. A second tawny, Chaya, first has only the right eye open, then manages both, her eyebrows working hard to wrest the lids apart. Wild Ramps gives a big blink, reclosing her right eye at the sight of this new world.

And it *is* a new world. For the world as a pup smells it in their first few weeks changes shape when they can see it, too—when the odor, which spreads in all directions, turns out to be navigable, explorable, and measurable.

All the opened puppy eyes are blue, the lightness of a tentative spring flower. My heart leaps at this striking color, but I know it won't last. For most dogs, blue is only the first color of their eyes—it is the color of new irises not yet darkened with melanin. The front of the iris, the stroma, will generally turn brown or hazel by the time they are adults. The pups' temporarily clear eyes feel like a fleeting gateway into who they are. It is the first moment that I feel that there is someone in there. And they are, it appears, looking back at us, starting to see us just as we see them. This observation is completely human of me, of course. Even with their eyes newly open, they cannot see much—they are heavily nearsighted—and the brilliant light of the world surely blitzes out any details they can see. Their brows are furrowed, their expressions much like what I expect I wear when just awakened and reluctantly encountering morning. But for us, the eyes are the window to the soul, the access point to the mind, the carrier of warmth and humor and gentleness. So it's the moment the puppy becomes a person.

Sight is not the only sense coming on line this week. I zoom in on one of the white puppies, Cranberry, whose snout is especially wrinkly and who twitches softly in sleep. Her ears are tiny triangles, each a small felt flap. Today they have flopped forward, covering the ear opening. This is the beginning of the possibility for the pup to notice noises from this bright new world. In another week the ears will be completely open. Their hearing will still be developing for several more weeks, but for now they can begin to register sounds. The literature on early dog vocalizations tells me that they cry and whine. But these words do not conjure up the range of noises rising from the pile. Sure, they cry and whine— exactly the noises that pups *should* make when they find themselves beached in outer space, far from their mother. The overall chorus of the puppy pile, though, consists of squeals; squeaks; various moans, groans, and moany groans; tiny bird squawks, chirps, and chatters; and the precise sound that you would expect a toy hyena would make. Most of these are mouth sounds, but the whine is a noise that comes from the nose, not just the mouth, giving it a special rumbly resonance. Happily, even puppy yawns make a (very small) sound.

Maize steps into the pen, panting lightly. She is keeping an eye on me but somehow manages not to step on any puppy tails. Soon a few swim her way—nearly crawling but bent under the weight of their great bobble heads. I stay still and quiet as Maize lies down and several pups begin to nurse.

🦴

Hundreds of miles south, there is another young litter, birthed by Pinto. One side of Pinto's trading card shows a photo of a slim, smiling dog; the other, her stats: date of birth, June 6, 2014; breed, Labrador retriever; job, human remains detection. Pinto has a trading card because she is a working dog, trained by the Penn Vet Working Dog Center, or WDC. And her job now is doubled. She is a mom to eight pups, seven female. They are sleekly black, the color of their dad, a search and rescue dog from Arizona with whom she was paired. Their puppies, too, are destined to be working dogs, trained generally to find people and odors, then placed where their skills lie and where they are needed.

In other words, they are destined for greatness. They will get an extraordinary amount of trainerly attention in their first year, quite different from most companion dogs. For now, though, they are one-week-old grubs living next to the kitchen in a house in Bryn Mawr, Pennsylvania. Alice and Keith, a nurse and physician, are fostering the litter for the birth—whelping—and early weeks. They are not dog trainers; they are just people who, like Amy, were ready to extend themselves to welcome chaos in the form of puppies in their early lives. In Alice's case, she started fostering working-dog litters after her mother passed away from ovarian cancer and she discovered the WDC's ovarian-cancer detection-dog-training program.

I see the litter for the first time at one week old. I FaceTime in, feeling like the grandmother video calling to see her grandchild— assessing how much of their development is due to their upbringing and how much to their dogness. I have met Pinto several times before, when she was only a year old, a svelte adolescent with soft eyes and energy more controlled than one would expect of an oversize puppy. And now I am surprised to suddenly be visiting her babies: the *V* litter, as the WDC calls them, for the first letter of their future names. For now, they are called by the colors of the bright collars that have already been placed around their necks: Yellow, Pink, Purple, Orange.

Look past the collars, though, and they look like any other litter. I cannot yet see, at this stage, that they are meant for working-dog greatness, that each will flourish with a different handler, detecting a different drug or disease or missing soul. They grunt small contented grunts and squeak creaky-rocking-chair squeaks when someone abruptly levitates them from the warmth of the pile.

I catch a glimpse of my image in the video call and find I am making ridiculous wide-eyed faces at them. Pinto wanders into the screen, keeping a worried eye on the person near her pups. She noses each of them in turn, counting them with her snout. At Orange she stops and delivers long body-cleansing licks to her belly, tongue outstretched measuring her length. The puppy submits completely, powerless before Big Tongue.

Puppies are born with relatively giant heads and broad foreheads; their eye orbits are large, and their mouths are wide. During their first weeks everything grows, but different parts grow at different rates—the mouth, or palate, gets longer much faster than it gets wider; the body grows faster than the head. By adulthood, the average dog has a long and narrow snout and a smaller forehead. That is an average, of course, and among the hundreds of dog breeds, there are examples on the extreme in either direction. Indeed, some—like the short-nosed, large-eyed French bulldog—are snapshots of early dog development: frozen in their puppylike shape.

This time in young puppy development is called the transitional stage, as they move out of the group self into themselves. And moving is part of it, literally. The tiniest movements of eyes, mouth, nose, and ears allow puppies to start to tune in to the world; movement of limbs allows pups to start exploring it. Each sound they hear, taste they collect, smell they sniff, and sight they see begins to shape them; their reactions toward—or away from or interacting with—each of those aspects of the world shape them further. Their limbs are filling with energy. Their tails are gearing up to wag. They begin tentative explorations, not fully upright but under their own steam. It takes days to get their front legs to move voluntarily, then more days for those legs to power them forward. The hind legs come on line several days later, so by twelve days old they are less swimming than they are wobbly crawl-walking. To be sure, their main preoccupations are still sleeping and nursing. But even their sleep is more animated now.

Just like humans, dogs are altricial, unable to care for themselves and dependent on parents for their very survival after birth. In other words, they are not fully developed in the uterus and need a little more time to get the entire body running smoothly. Pups, though, are on a radically speedier path than human babies. By this week in the puppies' lives, they will change from slow-moving, rooting potatoes to recognizable dogs.

While human babies are still trapped in their slowly developing bodies, puppy bodies are already ramping up key details. The eyes are opened; the ears are opening. The tongue starts tonguing; the voice starts voicing. With open eyes, dogs make a huge step into what will be the foundation of their bond with people: looking at, watching, and learning about us. Opened eyes allow for expressiveness—side-eyes, sleepy eyes, let's-go-for-a-walk eyes—as well as blinking. Dogs have, researchers determined, three spontaneous blink types: fully closed, half-closed, and one eye. On average, an adult dog will fully blink about thirteen times a minute—just about the rate of human blinking (but half the rate of the average gorilla and considerably more than the nearly nonblinking guinea pig). Dogs vary less in blink rate than in how quickly they reopen their eyes after the lid descends. Incredibly, this is detectable—and detected—by the adoring human eye. We rate those dogs who unblink most quickly as the most intelligent dogs.

With opening ears, puppies not only hear one another; they are also now able to be startled by sounds. Being startleable may not seem like a useful development, but it is one way that the world starts becoming perceptible to the newborn animal. Each puppy finds themself in a world abuzz, among fellow creatures, adding another layer to their growing understanding.

The tiny puppy tongue has a way of sticking just out of the mouth—a blep, in nonscientific terms—but it is more than just cute. While it will never work to help form speech sounds like the human tongue, dogs' considerable tongue musculature enables them to groom themselves; explore the taste of an object before ingesting it; and even, by curling backward, pull a column of water, adhering to the front of the tongue, neatly (okay, messily) into their mouths. It is full of capillaries to help in lowering body temperature when panting. But the tongue also winds up being used meaningfully in interactions with others (face licking is part of the most enthusiastic greetings of other dogs or people); as an investigative organ (licking a surface brings odor molecules to the vomeronasal organ, above the roof of their mouth, to be smelled); and as a sign of stress (the tongue flick, a short in and out of the tongue tip, is a clear signal of uncertainty or fear).

Their voices have grown louder and are getting more specific. Soon they will be listening to the world around them and barking back. Given that their closest relatives, gray wolves, rarely bark, it is thought that domestication brought out the bark in dogs. Indeed, a guard dog with a strong bark would be desirable. The many kinds of barks in every dog's repertoire are used in different contexts—from social play to when left alone—and have different meanings: as an alert, goad, warning, or plea. I bend down over the puppy pile, inhale a heady smell of milk, fur, and bodies, and try to hear what they're saying.

FEBRUARY ❋ WEEK 3
The Week of Poop

Three weeks into the pups' lives, I open the door to visit them, not knowing exactly what I'll find. The distinctive odor of many animals living in a small space greets me first. The warmth of the woodstove reaches my face as I shut the door on the winter chill.

The cockatoo losing all her back feathers side-eyes me warily; barking is in stereo.

In the puppy room Maize wags at me sweetly. She is just outside the pen with a cluster of puppies, and as I approach she pokes her head over the gate, almost visibly counting each of her offspring with her nose.

The pups are fat dumplings with tails, tossed in a heap. They groggily stir and stretch into awakeness, tumbling toward the mountainous figure looming over them and making high, friendly sounds. For the first time, they are sensing me. They may see me as more mountain than person; still, it is hard not to feel immediate gratification at being the focus of interest of these little dough-balls. Their interest is expressed in biting, mouthing, suckling, kneading. I squat down among them and experience the full onslaught. Mouth first, they lick my sleeve and one another, trying to take bites of my knees, grabbing a sibling by the head. This is the week their teeth have come in, and they seem fascinated by what they can now secure with their tiny mouth knives. My watchband is fully examined and tasted, at one point, by five puppies at once. At the pups' current size, my outstretched fingers can entertain three of them. Flint chomps my pinkie, Wild Ramps licks my ring, and Acorn rests his head on the other three digits. A new sound is coming out of a puppy somewhere in the jumble: a high, almost cartoonish squeal. If it were coming from a baby, we would be completely confident in translating the utterance as *ruh-roh*.

Maize looks around with worried eyebrows as her tidy bunch of puppies distributes itself around the pen. I find myself talking out loud to her puppies: "Oh, you're biting my finger!"; "You're a very fat one . . ." as I tickle Pawpaw's head; ". . . and you're a very little one," of the tiny Chaya. She's shivering, and I trace full, long warming strokes down her body with my hand. "Here's a yawning one"—Pumpkin—"and tiny lamb belly"—Cholla Cactus, lying on his back, pink limbs reaching upward, with ears and mouth flopped open. Persimmons starts nosing her way up the cuffs of my pants; Cranberry, the prodigious noisemaker of the litter, is whimpering. Even as I watch her, she adds some consonants to the whimper and suddenly comes out with the first legitimate bark I have heard. Wild Ramps sneaks behind me, worrying the heel of my shoe, and as if by prearrangement, Blue Camas takes on the other shoe. Fiddlehead is trying to get, as far as I can tell, inside my knee, mouth-first. There is a lot of puppyness happening.

They have definitely hatched this week, and the nest, such as it is, will soon be left. Trying to scale my legs, they claw over one another, stepping on heads, licking and mouthing anything in front of them, including one another's faces. Each movement is there in its rudimentary form: to climb, one must first paw at; to step, one must first lift a front leg off the ground. It is the next step where they falter, but they are not deterred long. The pure resilience to *keep at it* is present in each of them. I see a few tails gearing up to wag, managing only erratic, asymmetrical flits, as if the tail is not sure how to go both back *and* forth. It is also the week they have begun eliminating on their own: there are tiny poops on every surface and in every corner, and erratic golden lines that track where they've been while peeing—including on their siblings' backs. The reflex to eliminate has begun to mature, but the urge to eliminate at the edge of their own nest has another week in development.

All are much larger than the week before, except Chaya, whose fur is matted and who is not at all robust. Everyone's ears flop down, jiggling gaily with each tumble. They all have the wee pug nose, the flattish face; the fatter ones have rolls of skin forming around the eyes and nose. Their nails are also precociously sharp, I learn as one navigates up my jacket sleeve.

When Maize hops neatly into the pen, within seconds everyone stops what they are doing and heads mom-ward. As she stands, a few of the merles—and Cranberry, the largest—can just suckle while upright. I grab Chaya and direct her head to a swollen teat, holding her there as she drinks.

When Maize abruptly jumps out, the pups fall off. This week

she may begin weaning them from her milk, a process that takes one week or several, depending on the breed and the individual. I realize that it is just as their mom is starting to distance herself from them that the puppies have started to notice me—as though, ultimately, all movement, all behavior, is in search of mom, even as she just gets farther and farther away. With Maize's retreat, the puppies settle into a pile again, burrowing into and under one another, and are quickly asleep. There is a kind of puppy topography, the ways puppy hills and puppy valleys best fit together; which size pup can pile on the others; which precipice tumbles off, creating a new fault line. Their urge not just to be near but to be fully in contact with one or four others gives the lie to any dog-keeping that segregates a single dog from others and from people. It makes me want to reproduce that comfort for them.

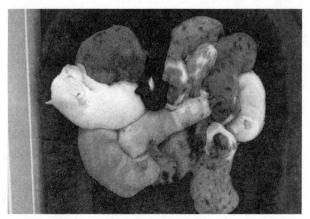

Puppy pile!!

At three weeks old the puppies have toddled into a key developmental period. This stage has been described as "the most influential nine weeks of a puppy's life." Until now their mother has been the sun around which their world revolves. She is the puppies' main source of food, warmth, and comfort; the one they talk to, they search for, they yearn to touch. For the next several weeks the puppies will be in a socialization period, or sensitive period, during which they are open to learning about everything that might be in their world. What they learn in these weeks is the foundation for growing up to be happy, healthy, well-adjusted adults; without this foundation, their happiness, health, and adjustment tuning can be challenging or unachievable. Indeed, the higher rate of behavioral disorders in commercially bred or puppy mill dogs is linked to insufficient stimulation during these weeks. These weeks lay the groundwork for how puppies deal with others socially and sexually, how they play and when they are aggressive, how and whom to imitate, what to fear, and when to explore. They form the basis of a pup's trainability and emotional stability—all the things that a new pup owner will encounter in the first days of living with them. It is when they learn to trust and bond with people or learn a suspicion of people. So, yeah, a big deal.

The Austrian ethologist Konrad Lorenz famously introduced the public to the idea of animals' "critical periods" of social development, during which the growing youngsters need exposure to others of their species to learn, essentially, how to be the animal that they are. Lorenz demonstrated both the flexibility and the rigidity of this period by making himself, and not an adult goose, the first large moving thing that a brood of young goslings saw when they hatched. While flexible enough to accept that a middle-aged Austrian was a model goose, they were not flexible enough to rethink that decision when he behaved more human than goosey. They followed him around dutifully, and he, in turn, took the geese on swimming expeditions, trying to help along their development into actual swimming birds. Alas, learning to fly was particularly tough with a land-bound model.

Unlike Lorenz's geese, puppies do not imprint rigidly on the first living thing they see. Instead, the socialization period lasts for several weeks. That it begins at about three weeks is not accidental. Their bodies are rapidly developing. At three weeks their nervous systems have matured enough for them to learn by association. With eyes and ears joining the other senses in transmitting information about the world, the sensory and motor cortices of the brain mature rapidly, helping to forge those connections between what they experience and what they do. Humans have a socialization period as well, but unlike dogs, who have gone through a transitional period of rapid development, human infants are still incredibly immature and completely dependent on their mothers. As a result, the infant's primary social figures are their caregivers; for dogs, the primary relationships will be with their siblings—or any other animals they encounter.

And I do mean *any* animals. For puppies the sensitive period of development is a time when they can be exposed not only to dogs but also to people, cats, rabbits, horses, cows—to any species with which they might need to peaceably interact—in order to impress the idea of their familiarity on the pup. Remove a puppy from their litter and raise them exclusively with sheep, and they will forge a relationship and way of interacting with sheep—treating them as normal social companions—that other puppies of their litter will not have. This is not to say that they will act like a sheep; they won't. They will act like a dog whose friends are all sheep-shaped. And, relatedly, they won't be as skilled in dealing with other dogs, or with people, if they didn't grow up with them. One researcher, Michael Fox, raised Chihuahua puppies with a cat and her kittens; when faced with a mirror, the pups did not wag, gaze, or bark at the image the way pups raised with their own litters do. Raised among felines, these Chihuahuas must not have recognized the odd-looking cat looking back at them. I don't think it has been done, but raise a puppy among porcupines, and you will get a porcupine-friendly adult. (I cannot vouch for the friendliness of the porcupines.)

The pups also have to learn to deal with one another now. Their littermates have transformed from warm sleep buddies to increasingly independent other beings. While they have long been aware of one another, they are now coming to a different level of awareness: of others as separate puppies. At this age they are perfectly able to recognize their siblings by smell, and if given the choice of lying on bedding with the odor of their siblings on it or bedding with the odor of an unknown pup, they choose to sleep with their siblings' smell. The first two weeks of living in and around one another, with no equipment to make an escape, creates a bond that makes the social experimentation of the coming weeks possible. All that biting of one another's body parts could be described as a safe, if poorly controlled, experiment on what happens when they bite. The reaction from some of their targets—biting back—is the beginning of learning to inhibit their own bites. Without this daily or even hourly experimentation and feedback, puppies might bite more forcefully as adults—too forcefully for most people and dogs they will encounter.

The socialization period is so named because it is the time pups can learn how to be social with other beings, but this time from three weeks to twelve or fourteen weeks is also when they can be exposed to new noises, smells, textures, contexts—"novel stimuli," as the research likes to call them. For a brief window, and provided that the novel stimulus is not too fearsome, puppies can learn to be okay with . . . just about anything. These weeks are the time to send out the Roomba and turn up the fans, to have strangers arrive at the door and ring the bell, to roller-skate by, to play playlists of city noise. And that is just what has begun under Amy's fostering. The radio, the birds squawking, the barks of other dogs in the background: the pups are getting nonstop exposure to these sounds—and will come to think of them as normal, not at all alarming. And I am part of that socialization. Every visitor gives the puppies a chance to learn about people in a safe context. But I am trying hard not to feel too special, because to the puppies, I am just a representative bipedal, hand-using, short-nosed animal who makes odd noises and has sleeves and cuffs for exploring, quite different from their siblings. They find me smellable, bitable, scalable, and lickable, like their littermates, but while I bring distinctive odors of my home, and my own way of handling and talking to them, I am not *me* to them. For now, I'll take it.

Meanwhile, in Bryn Mawr, the three-week-old *V* litter is watching action movies, volume on high. A noisy, busy vacuum runs regularly, and a hoverboard hovers by them. Their socialization is a heightened variation on the theme playing out with Maize's pups: exposure to new and possibly bizarre phenomena, as well as to people of all sorts. Their foster family has three kids in the house, and they have just begun letting older and younger visitors in to meet the pups. "Anything I can find with wheels gets rolled by the pen," foster mom Alice tells me. The whelping pen is right where breakfast is served, by the kitchen, so the pups can hear, see, and smell all its goings-on. Next week they will get a visit from the Working Dog Center researchers.

FEBRUARY ❧ WEEK 4
Professional Wag

Wander into a store in the United States catering to parents of babies and young children, and you're likely to find a child activity gym among the products to amuse and educate little ones. It consists of a mat with a few plastic or wooden rods doming above it, from which hang various objects of ostensible interest to a baby: a rattle, colorful shapes or animal figures, something pullable or ringable. When my son, Ogden, was a baby, he was attracted to dangling bells and rattles that he could try to kick, hit, or grab to make a pleasing racket.

What the designers of these gyms probably did not have in mind was their use by four-week-old puppies. And by *use* I mean "invasion and destruction." When ten-year-old Ogden and I arrive at Amy's this week, the puppies and their new equipment—beds, a litter box, various pull and chew toys designed for dogs—have completely displaced the living room furniture, which is huddled along one wall. Among the pups' new possessions is an infant activity gym in the primary colors typical of early-childhood toys. Blue Camas is playing the part of the baby in the gym, except she is knocking into the toys with her head and body, then moving to bite the offending dangler. A furry green caterpillar knocks her over; on the ground, she discovers she has a tail and moves to bite it, too.

It makes sense to have an activity gym for the puppies, because this is the week that their activity blossoms. In addition to the gym, Amy has provisioned their space with a short tunnel made of rings and nylon. Soon this is the place to look if you are counting puppies and one seems to be missing. And soon Ogden and I provision the space with ourselves, stepping into the pen and sitting down to be wrangled with. Six squeaks come to meet me, some underestimating their speed or our distance and running squarely into my shins. They are now the size of sturdy loaves of bread—only with stumpy limbs. They are toddling, walking as if wearing shoes two sizes too large. Wild Ramps lurches by, her tail radiantly wagging—the most coordinated part of her. Their tail wags now alternate between loosely sweeping, merry oscillations and divining rods; tails vibrating lightly and curved, helping to hold their pudgy bodies upright. The tail tips are tiny exclamation points at the end of their bodies. Edible ones, apparently: I regularly see a puppy reach for a nearby sibling's tail and start gnawing on it.

Maize is nearby, her ears back, her tail marking an interested but concerned beat, her belly still swollen down to her knees. The puppies continue their daily pattern of going between pile sleeping and awakeness, but that awake time is now less about finding mom's belly than about exploring the space. Or maybe it is just that they can less often find her belly: she is no longer lying helpfully on her side, enabling breakfast, lunch, dinner, and several in-between snacks. While they are still nursing daily, Amy has begun giving the puppies a canned puppy food—the WDC puppies' trainers call it *gruel*—delivered in a circular tray so that each puppy forms a ray of the sun.

I toss two long purple pull toys among the little loaves, giving each a shake as I do. The objects in the pen explicitly designed as dog toys do not seem to register with the puppies very much. While we look at a rope tug or squeaky ball and sense its function immediately, it is far less interesting to the puppies than the edge of the dog bed on which they lie or a finger near their faces. With much persistence Ogden encourages Persimmons to grab on to the tiniest of red tennis balls, which she finally does, cooperatively gripping it in her mouth like an old pro. Then we realize that she is frozen in place and may simply not know how to release it.

Ogden gently removes the ball from her mouth, and she toddles on her way. Instead of toys I have brought keys. I pull out my largest key chain, holding keys for long-forgotten locks, and abruptly drop it on the floor beside me. Its clanking causes all the humans to look toward me, eyebrows questioning, but none of the puppies. A sudden novel noise disturbs them not at all: it is only the way the world is to them—noises happen, hands lift, bodies bang. Without yet any sense of how the world *should* be, their world can be anything at all.

There are other human visitors in the pen today, and we each sit cross-legged or with our legs spread in a V, both of which in puppy language are apparently invitations. We trade hosting seven or more puppies at a time. Just as their rate of chewing one another's faces and small bits has escalated, they now pile on one another more forcefully. There is regularly a puppy completely plopped over another, or a tiny head poked out from under three healthy rumps. Unusually, Amy's calico cat hops into the pen. She may be looking for the couch now crowded with puppies. She wanders among them, sniffing a few closely; Acorn opens an eye but is not excited into action. The puppies may just be tired, but they barely pursue her. When one does extend a paw to her head, she neatly leaps up to the top of the wobbly gate lining the pen and takes her leave of them.

I have started to interpret what each puppy does as indicative of their character, though I know I am seeing only the briefest glimpse. Some are more talkative, some more bold—but this might reflect different rates of development. Distinct personalities will not truly shine through for a couple of weeks. Still, there are behavioral differences to see: Wild Ramps and Pawpaw lie in repose on their backs, little legs shot up in the air, and allow us to tickle their warm bellies. Fiddlehead wobbles over and starts gnawing Wild Ramps on the elbow. Flint has a kind of natural smile in sleep. Persimmons lets Amy plop her on her lap and trim her claws without complaint; Pumpkin arrives everywhere mouth open, looking to bite. I watch him fall asleep with his mouth completely open, midchomp on Chaya's face. Amid the cacophony I sit grinning widely, pleased to be in their growing world. It is an unmatched pleasure to be the subject of a four-week-old puppy's gaze, or even mouth—even though I know not to take it personally. They are equal-opportunity agreeable, including to a ten-year-old boy whose idea of how you might pick up a puppy is different from that of the fifty-year-olds' in the room.

୫୨

Finally able to maintain their own body temperature at a canine-normal 101.5 degrees, the puppies do not have to stay huddled with one another all the time. So they are exploring, taking advantage of their rapidly improving senses and mobility to introduce themselves to new things. With perception comes movement, and with movement comes contact with the world. Each week the puppies' world expands.

While it is just wrong to say, as scientists used to, that puppies do not explore until four weeks of age, the ferocity of their exploration has ramped up. Two weeks ago it was still mostly restricted to the distance between the puppy pile and their mother; last week it was the far reaches of their pen; this week it is creatures coming into their pen, some of whom purr or emit a fog of smelly sounds from their mouths. This week the world includes things that are above their heads, things they can move into or grab hold of.

The essence of life is movement. On a small scale, within their bodies, neural connections are forming in their brains, routines of sensation and action becoming established. And on a grand scale, their bodies' movement in space. This week the puppies are learning the size and extent of their bodies, the results of their mouthing and pawing, the feel of different substances underfoot.

And these are just the things that puppies should be introduced to at this time: the pieces of their lives to be. The sounds they will hear, of nature and of human society. We all talk to the puppies, but we are also introducing them to the sounds of our movement and the sounds of our objects, from phones that squawk, to chairs that screech on the floor, to vehicles whose engines roar abruptly. The animal and people smells they will smell—everything from the cleaner with which we wash the floor, to the food we will provide them, to human body odor. The feelings they will feel—including, most critically, people touching them, picking them up, grabbing their tails or paws. Having their nails trimmed is a dozen experiences at once: being held in place, on their backs, pressed up against a person; the stretch of each toe away from the other, the sharp smell and sound of the clippers, the rippling sensation radiating into their toes from the snip. Someone is squeezing their paws—likely the first time anyone has grabbed their feet—and cooing, talking, exhaling at them, inches from their face. After this immersion, a young pup probably needs a little nap.

With open eyes they have spent the last weeks starting to focus their gaze. Part of the reason the puppies may not have been terribly keen on the dog toys in their pen is that they are just developing depth perception, which allows them to integrate information from each eye into a three-dimensional form. Without depth perception, it is hard to grab at anything at all: the world may be rich with colors and light, but it is flat. By the time they are four weeks old, though, puppies have been found to have excellent depth perception.

At this stage, where one pup goes, the others are likely to follow. Siblings are now one another's biggest teachers. Much of their group exploratory behavior happens because one pup sniffs this, digs that, picks up this other thing—and their siblings do what they do. This social facilitation enables them to find safe foods to eat and figure out what is chewable, benefiting from their brother's or sister's experience. Just as their digestive systems are maturing and they can defecate more intentionally, Amy has put a large tray, similar to a cat's litter box, by the activity pen. While many puppies walk around it or just trounce through it heedlessly, some stop and use it. When one does, others are drawn to the scene and sometimes use it, too. Ta-da: housebreaking, step one.

The puppies are wandering and wagging, and their wagging tails are in fact a major advancement. They are using them actively for the first time: a fifth appendage is exceptionally helpful in providing balance. Shortly, the tail wag will be a useful signal to other dogs, expressive of emotion and intent. Naturally short-tailed pups, with only six tail bones, use their tails to communicate just as the twenty-three-boned long-tailed dogs do. As for us tailless bipeds: it is hypothesized that just *seeing* a puppy tail is rewarding for humans. I know a wagging tail can change my mood. *Why don't humans have tails?* I wonder, watching a puppy's black tail, dipped in white and curling at the end, quiver as she pokes her head into my jacket pocket. A certain sign of dogs' evolution past humans.

🦴

One-month-old working dogs are developing in just the same way. The *V* litter, destined to be hero dogs in their future, are snoring on a soft blanket when Jenny Essler, a researcher from the Working Dog Center, arrives. She tries to rouse them: "Hi, puppies! What are you doing? Pup-pup-pup-puppy!" Today Jenny has brought what she describes as "random things for them to start climbing and to feel weird things under their feet" and a catnip toy for them to try to track. "They are tracking it with the smell way more than with their eyes at this age," she explains.

Each puppy is awakened by being lifted out of their pen. Placed on a blanket, the pups yawn lazily as they take stock of the situation. Jenny is waving the catnip toy in front of their faces. They are slow to track it. Yellow looks blankly in its direction and stumbles toward it after a long delay. Another experienced trainer, Dana Ebbecke, brings out a camera and squeaks a toy to get the pup's attention; she is not rewarded with their attention. Blue is a little more interested in the toy, starting to grab at it . . . before losing focus. Red struggles forward, making whimper-gurgly sounds. The trainers offer a stream of reassurances and commendations— "Good girl! You're up! Look at your paws! You're down! Helloooooo! Bop-bop-bop-bop-bop! Hey, good morning!" Jenny tells me that when they interview intern candidates at the WDC, they ask, *Can you be silly?* because you can't be straight-faced while training dogs.

Purple has especially big feet and a tiny shar-pei face, which scrunches up even more as the trainers handle her paws to get her used to the sensation. As a working dog in training, she may wind up having to navigate over rubble to find human survivors after a building collapse or to endure hours of being patient, waiting alone, between episodes of intense work. Many of the working dogs will be put into dangerous situations that most dogs would reasonably avoid. In a way, Jenny says, "we're training really 'stupid' dogs—in that we're training them to do things that are unsafe, that they shouldn't want to do." But they are also training them to trust the humans who bring them to those places, who will not send their dogs in to do something that they are not prepared to do. And that trust begins now, on the floor in Bryn Mawr, with Jenny on her hands and knees, gazing into a puppy face gazing back at her, and cooing.

MARCH ❋ WEEK 5
Mouths with Tails

Teeth of five-week-old puppies are quite sharp. As I step into their pen, multiple puppies attack me by climbing on and biting all my parts. The pant leg, the snap of a jacket, the hair untucked around an ear. Toe of shoe, heel of shoe, shoelaces (a special delicacy). They bite the air around me, an invisible image of me extending two inches in all directions. No one got my nose, but that was because of many high-speed maneuvers performed under fire that kept some small portion of me unbitten.

They aim their mouths toward anything new or near, so each movement I make is a mouth attractant. As I reach to pet Pumpkin, he nips my hand. I pretzel my legs in sitting, and Cranberry dives into that negative space and chews her way out from under my leg. Fiddlehead climbs my shirt and finds an earlobe. Thank you, Fiddlehead, for nibbling. I begin to feel defined by the parts that have been investigated by a puppy mouth.

For young dogs, as for young humans, the mouth is the first organ of exploration: the way they discover what's what, who's who, and what what's made of. For parents of toddlers, this means making their world safe for mouth creatures: covering open outlets, putting away any objects—marbles, Lego bricks, pennies—

that could fit in a young mouth until they grow out of this stage of development. For parents of toddling puppies, this means making their world safe for mouth creatures *forever*. They never stop being mouth creatures.

The resident cat steps into the pen with me, and I no longer am a person of interest; the puppies aim their mouths cat-ward. Watching them, I try to imagine going through life mouth-first. It is alarmingly intimate. As if to see an object we had to run at it, eyes wide, and make unflinching contact, smooshing it into our eyeballs.

The pups, of course, have no hesitation about the smoosh. For those of us with more reluctance about being explored by mouth, it is easy enough to proffer a tiny toy. The dog toys have reached the pups' consciousness this week. Pawpaw comes upon a ball and starts kicking it to himself. Acorn and Flint are doing their best to dismantle the activity gym by pulling on the toys until they snap. When Maize appears by my shoulder and pokes her head over the side of the pen, three puppies leap toward her, licking at her mouth. One turns around and finds my mouth, too, getting in a couple of quick licks as I sputter in surprise.

In body and behavior, the puppies seem much older than a week ago. They are chunky bunnies, pushing their way through the air and anything in the air in their way. All their tails are wagging. Everyone's ear flaps are floppy, and their eyes are transitioning out of blue. Most of their noses have gone from pink, through splotchy, to all black. The biggest pups have been caught up to, though the littlest still looks almost like a different species. Pawpaw has grown into the rolls on his face, but when Pumpkin or Cranberry lies down, you can see the extra skin just hanging off them. Acorn has a few sprouts beginning on his chin that might be furnishings—longer strands of hair growing around the eyebrows and muzzle.

At this age their ear canals are fully open. Finally the whispers and echoes haunting them have begun to transform into meaningful sounds. Heads turn at a distant clatter. They use sounds with one another: squeaking at the biter of their snout, the stepper on their tail. A few are working on a pretty serious bark. I brought a squeaking toy with me, a long purple tube that I bring to life with a pinch. It has the effect of bringing a moment of stillness and alertness to ten puppies. All but Cranberry. She is a pretty good producer of sounds herself—indeed, the most continual vocalizer of the group, whining regularly. But it appears that she is not receiving any word back. Amy was the first to think that Cranberry might be deaf. To look at her, one might guess she would be deaf. She is fully white, her eyes still more blue than the others. As unlikely as it might seem, there is a genetic connection between her eye and fur colors and her ears: the absence of the pigment-producing cells can lead to the underdevelopment or death of sensory cells in the ear.

Wild Ramps heads for the corner of the room, where she handily pushes herself through a doggy door, a small outlet cut into the house's back door with a movable flap that allows dog-size animals to push their way in or out. Outside! Just yesterday was the first day Amy let them out the back door onto a deck. Now the door flaps again and again as the puppies follow her; the whole lot exits, then enters, then exits. An action or idea or mood that strikes one ripples through the rest. So as Wild Ramps, while masticating a toy, tumbles into sleep, suddenly nearly all the pups follow. Within a minute all are head to tail to tail in a circle on a soft bed, asleep. Even in dreaming, though, they are alert to the world: when a dog barks nearby or a door opens, all but one lift their heads immediately.

Though they are still very puppyish, at this age they have taken another step in growing out of puppyhood: they are mostly weaned off their mother's milk. Living in human households, dog moms are free to wean at this age because there is a nearby person to take over feeding. For a few weeks Amy has been diligently introducing the puppies to a highly aromatic, very soft wet food and also giving Maize time alone, away from the puppies. Remarkably, something similar occurs among dogs not living in human households.

What we might think of as a "stray" dog, or a dog without a home, is generally considered a "free-ranging" dog if they in fact live their lives without a human home. This is not to say they live entirely without humans: free-ranging dogs live *around* humans, usually in well-populated areas, since they rely on the resources accidentally or intentionally provided by people in the form of trash or leftovers. They live in small social groups, described as loosely structured—meaning individual dogs may come and go—but they do form long-term relationships. Researchers observing free-ranging mother dogs in West Bengal, India, found that after the third week of their puppies' lives, lactating mothers begin to wean, and their female relations—grandmothers, aunts, and sisters—take over some of the care of the pups. These allomothers actually nurse the pups, as well as regurgitate food for them to eat, and generally keep an eye out that no pup wanders off or goes hungry. Some of these allomothers have their own litters and are sharing a little of their extra milk; others seem to spontaneously produce milk. (The occasional male contributes with his own regurgitation.) Not only does this cooperation allow mothers to start to leave the dens for longer periods to search for food themselves, it helps the litters survive.

The pups who leaped at Maize's mouth, licking and mewling plaintively—these pups were instinctively requesting that she might provide food from her mouth. A straight line can be drawn from this puppy request for mom to regurgitate a snack to the adult dog jumping up and licking a human face. Once a request, later a greeting; always happy with whatever comes out.

Not only does a change in diet begin to challenge the puppies' digestive systems, it provides a good primer in dog social cues. For when the puppies try to nurse now, their mother often scolds them—biting gently, growling, baring her teeth, generally telling them to skedaddle. But what a lesson! Mom is gently kicking them to the next level of maturity, using some of the same communications that they are sure to encounter as they bumble through the world of Other Dogs. Pups do learn to, in fact, skedaddle or show submissive, appeasing behavior, such as licking or rolling on their backs—or the scolding gets sharper.

Interaction with their littermates has escalated, providing constant social feedback as well. They have begun to see their siblings as playmates and mentors—imitating their new play moves and following them into new places and situations. Social play is the context for rapid learning about how to interact with others and discover their bodies' strengths and abilities, even one another's minds. Two puppies playing together cooperatively rapidly match and respond to behaviors. They bite but softly: siblings continue to be good practice for learning an inhibited bite. Pups weaned too early tend to be less skilled at this, and their siblings tell them so.

As they begin to follow each other to new sights, sounds, and smells, any fear they have of this or that thing can be buoyed or diffused by the reaction of the other puppies. Faced with a scary sight—like, say, a large man with a big hat—if one puppy toddles gaily toward him, the others often follow. They do not follow just any pup. They know who their siblings are. Five-week-olds placed in a cage with their siblings or what researchers called "alien pups" (here just meaning nonsiblings, not extraterrestrial pups) reliably approach their siblings first. With one exception—red setter pups were just exuberantly excited in all directions and did something more like *running manically around* than *approaching puppies carefully.*

Now that they are using them less often to nurse, their mouths are even freer to explore the environment. They are not trying to eat everything; they are trying to see everything by putting their mouths on objects. Perceiving an object depends not just on what it looks, smells, or feels like but also on how one can interact with it. Researchers put very willing dogs—including pups named Daisy, Ollie, and Truffles—in MRI scanners and showed them pictures or short video clips of objects (like a lime-green toy) that they had previously been trained either to mouth or to paw. If it was an object they had held in their mouths, a specific part of the brain that processes and identifies objects was much more active. So was the part that anticipates actions—suggesting that one of the ways dogs think about objects is, *Can I fit it in my mouth?*

The puppies' brains are rapidly maturing. With all their senses now up and running, connections are forged between sensory areas of the brain and areas involved in not just movements but also emotions. With fully working ears, puppies can be startled by a new category of things—loud, unusual, or surprising noises—and some even develop new fears. This is the time, indeed, when phobias—or what are called fear responses—to a category of object or a context might pop up. People are one of those object categories. Puppies who do not see and interact with humans from this age through the end of the socialization period can acquire a lasting wariness of people. While not impossible to overcome later, such mistrust could be completely averted by simply having friendly and gentle humans mixing it up with them when the puppies are young. It is as though the puppies' systems are particularly raw and sensitive now: everything that happens draws a deep groove in their psyches, one that is long lasting. Ideally, this is the age at which dogs are gradually exposed to a growing number and diversity of phenomena in order to avoid any fearful grooves.

This is exactly why the *V* litter trainers arrive this week and the next with a metal cookie sheet, a wet towel, and an Altoids tin half-full of pennies. The puppies still wear their colored collars to help distinguish them, but they have also been named: Vita, Villa, Vig, Victoria, Vega, Vaz, Vara, Vauk. Taking advantage of the puppies' increasing coordination between what they see and where they go, the trainers flit a toy in front of Purple's—now Vaz's—face. Vaz, who's been napping, groggily tracks the toy, sniffing nonstop in a slow-motion pursuit. She stretches her neck as far as she can without moving her rump but eventually gets up. She is led onto the cookie sheet, covered with a wet towel to keep her from slipping. They lead her back and forth without a hiccup. For the trainers it is a success, exposing her to a weird texture and sensation; for Vaz, it is just the way the world is.

When not being led around on cookie sheets, the puppies, just like Maize's litter, are mostly sleeping. When they decide on sleep, they are deeply committed to it. They can be roused again, but it is clearly the time of some important growth.

The next week's testing advances the challenges the slightest bit. The trainers toss a rattle tin can at the pups, tease them with a cat toy on the end of a pole, and stick them up on a wobbly tabletop to see how they react. Jenny voices her assessments of each one. "You're a funny one . . . Not the best grip, but she's got spunk . . . She's got a good grip: you might get puppy of the day." Vaz is wide-awake this week, her tail wagging like crazy. She grabs the cat toy and shakes her head forcefully to tear it apart. "You're a little scoundrel, aren't you?" After her set of challenges, Vauk (formerly Green) sits right down and looks around, her tail wagging gently. The bravest puppy ever! Yes, you are.

MARCH ❀ WEEK 6
Little Bruisers

Meeting eleven six-week-old puppies is a protracted exercise in replacing your body parts with dog toys in their mouths. Being overtaken with puppies is like being tickled: right on the edge between delicious and terrifying. They have no sense of personal space, no feeling that we shouldn't be in contact with each other in every possible way. The very silky coats of the young puppies have started to roughen on some, but many are still beautifully soft. They smell sharp: both mildly sour, like milk that has gone bad, and feral, like the smell you just catch in the forest of a wolf that has passed the night before. I can't help but smell them, of course, because when I sit, they are immediately in my face. They head for my mouth and nose. I have had puppies chew my curls.

This is what I expect when entering the House of Puppies. Instead, today I hear a roar of silence. The only sounds are of my own movement and breath, my footfalls echoing brightly.

The spell is broken by a chorus of barks coming from the large meadow behind Amy's house. I hurry to the back door and see the puppies outside, in a smaller fenced area. They are milling around, poking their noses into the wind. This is the first time I have seen them all outdoors: their smallness in the natural world is surprising. Even while small, they are beautifully tubby balled socks of puppies. Little bruisers. They have grown into their skin, and personalities are popping into their visages. Chaya has a gentle, sweet face, reminiscent of a piglet. Cranberry, who has a blue sparkle remaining in her eye, has an earnest look, eyes at half-mast as though blind instead of deaf. The spotted dogs are distinguishing themselves from one another: Flint has a becoming look, with a broad white flash down his forehead between his eyes and one black eye; Pawpaw has two black eyes, giant ears, and is growing a beard. Difference between sexes has begun to emerge: all the girls are smaller than the boys.

I have brought my whole family along this time, wanting to let them in on the full puppy experience. Ogden and my husband, Ammon, should have been coming with me all along, I realize: it's the type of encounter they enjoy completely, while my approach is to analyze and worry. Ammon is the kind of fellow who stops to talk to every dog on the sidewalk, often kneeling to vigorously pet them and let them snuffle into his face and hair. For his part, Ogden delights in warning Ammon about puppy teeth and puppy claws and puppies all up in your face—while willingly lying down to subject himself to their attack.

Ammon steps into the pen first, and even as he swings his leg over the fence, he is mobbed by puppies, a magnet to whom they are uncontrollably attracted. They zoom to his ankles and clamber over one another to get to his shins and knees. As he tentatively moves forward, they move with him. When Ogden steps in, his own magnetism draws the closest ones over: puppies piling on one another to reach higher on his body.

Distinctive personalities are on full display now. There is the puppy who is always first to get napping, the one who cries a lot, one who pursues small flying insects, another who will hold on to the rope tug toy put in his mouth. And there are behaviors that are consistent across all puppies. None hesitate at the new feeling of dirt and grass on their soft pink toe pads—although only a few realize the pleasure of digging. Amy has put out various new objects, including a small flexible tunnel and a doghouse. These things do not register with the pups at all; they walk by them with nary a glance. But a tarp placed over a hole in the fence and flapping in the breeze draws several of the pups near and inspires a brand-new, freshly minted bark from one of them—more "bark" than bark. Movement captures their interest; peculiarly, most objects made to entertain dogs are motionless.

As completely enraptured as they seem to be by the flapping tarp and human magnets, when Amy pulls out what looks like a fishing rod with a squirrel dangling from it, everyone abandons us. It is a flirt pole—a lightweight rod with a clump of synthetic fur attached by a string off one end. Amy whips the pole around neatly and begins fishing for puppies. She catches four straight-away, and they hold on tight, marching like toy soldiers with the fur in their mouths.

We stay for hours, enough time to see the puppies cycle

through two rounds of high activity and sudden collapse into sleep. When Ogden sits on the ground, six puppies beeline to him and fall asleep on his lap and one another; he must keep his arms in a wide embrace to support their heavy heads. As I approach him quietly, not wanting to disturb his lapful, I hear a low murmuring sound. Suddenly I realize the source of the sound. It is the puppies, grunting contentedly as they exhale into sleep.

In the car on departure, two of us put our heads together and close our eyes, making puppy noises in sleep.

෪

Scientists recently got interested in dogs not because of their wagging tails or sweet smell, but because of their skill at social cognition—that is, their ability to learn from others to solve problems. One of the very first studies in the field now described as *dog cognition* aimed to see what adult pet dogs would do when a nearby human pointed to an overturned cup. For fellow humans, it is obvious what to do if faced with a scenario like this: look at the cup. It is so obvious that we do not even think about it; we just look. Depending on our motivation and curiosity, we might then approach the cup, look under the cup; if there is nothing there, we get that pointing human to explain themself. Human babies of ten months can at least do the looking, earlier than they can go over to the cup on their own: their brains work faster than their muscle coordination develops.

The task for the dogs in that study is to try to find a bit of hidden food. Every dog person knows that dogs can locate the tiniest crumb in a deep jacket pocket, so the question is not *if* they can find it. The question is if they can find it *our* way—by looking to others for clues. And, mostly, the dogs do: they will follow that point, knock over that cup, and gobble up whatever is underneath. In fact, at a certain age they will follow a person's guidance on which of two overturned cups has a treat underneath, even over the advice of their own noses. Given how often people point at things and how seldom they encourage dogs to smell things out (or to smell at all), this makes some sense. If they're living with us, we want them to follow our cues about where and what to eat, not just hunt through the house for every fallen crumb.

It turns out that this tendency to follow a human's pointing is not just a brilliant strategy if a dog lives with humans—it comes built into the dog. In one study, nearly 80 percent of six-week-old puppies were already able to follow a point to find which of two cups had a hidden treat. Even more could figure it out when a person placed a special marker on one of the cups, serving as an identifying clue.

By this age, puppies in most contexts will have had at least minimal exposure to people. While there are dogs who are *called* pointers, dogs do not generally point. So puppies' success at reading a completely different species' gesture as a form of communication is impressive and indicates that the ability to learn to understand pointing is genetic. They get better at point following over time and can even follow brief point gestures, finger-only points, and points across the body and in other odd arrangements— demonstrating that experience helps, too.

But there is another major cognitive leap that the puppies have made this week that is folded into the pointing study. *Object permanence* is more or less what it sounds like: an understanding that objects of all sorts continue to exist even when you cannot see them. It is a useful understanding to have, but it is not an ability that we seem to have when we are born. When young humans and other animals first come into the world, they experience a fluid, shifting landscape, in which objects disappear when they go out of sight or "out of smell." But six-week-old puppies? They get it. They know that objects should remain where they were left—even when they cannot be seen. Next time, take note of where your dog buries a bone/toy/particularly good stick in a yard or on a walk: they will search for it there when you pass by the site again.

In addition to their cognitive development, Maize's puppies are also showing something that's harder to see in science, where subjects' data gets summed and averaged: the importance of individual differences. There is no "average" Maize puppy; every pup is already toddling their own path. Some play tug with a rope toy; others chase insects. While science looks for the characteristics dogs have in common, what may be most interesting are their differences.

MARCH ❧ WEEK 7
Adventure Pups

"We're going on an adventure!" Amy announces as the puppies all tumble out the dog door onto the deck. For the first time, the dogs are going into the Big Yard. The Big Yard is acres of rolling land, mud piles, and a pond. It is bigger than the puppies' imagination. Two of Amy's adult dogs run circles around us, deftly leaping over the wee ones and taking advantage of the moment I crouch to tie a shoelace to jump on or over me. Most of the pups run after us, but Chaya, alone among the pups, hangs back by the fence. The rest rush headlong into the yard. They run in fits and starts, some alone and some in tandem, the larger dogs whipping around them. The smaller ones look admiringly at the doings of the bigger dogs, but when one runs too close or nips at them, the puppies are quick to dive and roll onto their backs, feet pedaling the air.

We head toward the pond, recently released from winter's grip. The three large adult dogs launch themselves in from the banks. Their activities draw a few of the puppies pondside. Fiddlehead sticks a paw in, quite by accident, pulls it quickly out, examines it, then places it in again, more gently. It did not do what she thought, and, looking surprised, she retreats. Pawpaw gets both paws in, as befits his name, and stands happily knee-high in pond muck. Other puppies approach the high bank (high to puppies) surrounding the pond, but beat a hasty retreat, rumps in the air and tails fully straight as if pointing their way to safety.

That the outside world comes in not just solid and air but liquid is a new idea for these little brains. At seven weeks old, the workings of their rapidly developing nervous system are visible in their behavior. Their interest in the new is what draws them pondside; their increasing hesitation about new things makes the visit short. While none will jump in the pond, even the shyest will jump on one another—and now will do so for the sheer enjoyment of it. They play with no goal in mind, with no winner or loser; it is pure energy in the shape of dogs.

Maize is out on a long leash, her movement restricted, as she has become increasingly irritable and impatient with her growing social companions. The puppies find her leash extremely tuggable. When they tire of that, they head for her belly, and for what turns out to be the last time, I watch them noisily gather in her shade and try to nurse. Only about a half dozen can fit their heads between her limbs. One can see, as they noisily and violently try to suck out any remaining milk, why Maize might be irritable.

When she starts walking, she sloughs them off, and they fan out in search of other pastimes. The adult dogs are the source of new fascination. This week marks the blossoming of the puppies' ability to learn from the older dogs, whose every move models possible behaviors and whose responses to the puppies are felt deeply and personally. They investigate the pond because the big dogs did; they follow them to an old firepit, to a gap in the fence. They jump on the dogs as they see them jumping on one another—and when scolded with a snarl, they cry out and fly toward me, tails low.

They have much more energy and endurance than even last week, but after an hour they start to tire. Flint heads toward me as I squat low, giving me a great sleepy wag. Fiddlehead runs to and then under me, having gotten a nip from a passing big dog. In their winding down they cycle through all their climbing and chewing tricks. I get my nose nipped, my finger gnawed; my knees and ankles are as delicious as ever. Shortly, several puppies are asleep on my shoes and between my knees. Wild Ramps sits out in the field, back to me, watching the world pass by.

Once puppies start recognizing other dogs as "like them," they gain a great skill: the ability to learn from them. Miniature dachshund puppies as young as twenty-eight days were set up to watch a puppy nearby use a ribbon to pull a small cart with food on it to within mouth reach. While it had taken the original group of puppies many minutes to figure out how to do this, after watching the demonstration the observing puppies solved it quickly—some within five seconds. I see evidence of this social learning in the Big Yard, where the older dogs' mere presence draws the pups to the pond; I can see this in their play together, when an adult gently chides an overenthusiastic puppy or a sibling bites a biter back. This transmission of information about how to engage with the world—about how to be a dog—can come from parents, from unrelated adults, or from peers.

Social learning has been researched in adult dogs, and there is plenty of evidence now that dogs not only can imitate others' actions but can understand the idea of imitation generally. Researchers in Hungary have demonstrated that dogs can learn to "do as I do"—to repeat *any (reproducible) action* that a person demonstrates. Training might start with teaching a dog to follow simple bodily actions—lying down, touching a hand (paw) to a box—done by a person. Once the dog has the gist, the human demonstrator can then try a completely novel action, like opening a book or pulling a wagon. Dogs who have learned to generally "do as someone has done" will come up with some way to open the book and pull the wagon themselves.

What of puppies, though, who have much less experience with others and who are not in any sense trained? Before knowing what imitation is, they show signs of being able to imitate. One study tested the behavior of Italian and Hungarian puppies of this age on opening a puzzle box—simply a closed box that requires some work to open. One box had a lid that needed to be lifted open; the other had a lid that could be slid to the side. The motivation for figuring out this puzzle of the closed box was that each held delicious, smelly food inside. One group of pups was set up so that they could watch an adult dog solve each puzzle a couple of times; another group of pups watched a person open the boxes.

A control group of puppies had no demonstrations at all, just got to puzzle the problem out themselves.

In the control group the puppies went at the boxes, pawing and chewing and puzzling, but after two minutes, fewer than half had figured out how to get at the food. But in the groups that watched a dog or a person open the box, over twice as many solved the puzzle—most in less than twenty seconds.

The accomplishment of these puppies was not just getting themselves a bit of food. It was showing that, just over a month after becoming able to see at all, they could already interpret others' actions as about something. The puppies saw the demonstrations as the means to the food, the way to act. And the pups could do one better: they could translate what they observed someone else doing into what they themselves needed to do. Even if the demonstrator was a person and used a hand—a body part that dogs do not in fact have—puppies figured out the mapping from hand to paw and manipulated the lid with their own paw/hand.

There was one exception to the puppies' imitative abilities. Those pups who watched their mothers do the demonstration were able to open the puzzle box only as well as the control group, those pups who had not seen a demonstration at all. While a litter's mother is formative in their development not just during gestation but for several weeks after birth, when her pups are nearing two months, her role is changing. Pups now receive much more scolding from mom for nursing, for stepping close to her, for making noise. Dog moms appear to play little role in their pups' lives after two months. This may be one reason the pups do not see her as one of the kinds of demonstrators—dog or person—to watch carefully.

This beginning of separation of the mother and her pups is seen most profoundly when there is no human around to swoop up the puppies and take them away. In free-ranging dog groups, parents stay with their pups for the first couple of months of their lives: dads guarding the litters from strangers of any species for six or eight weeks, and moms for up to three months. Thereafter, the dogs tend to disperse.

Owned dogs, of course, tend to disperse by being distributed to new owners. Most dogs living with humans will not see their mothers again. But this is not to say that they forget them. When two-year-old dogs, separated from their mothers at eight to twelve weeks of age, were given a choice of two towels to lie on, one of which had the odor of their mom and the other of an unknown dog, they recognized the scent of their mother, spending more time with the mom towel. Similarly, long after litters have scattered, mothers spend more time sniffing the towels impregnated with the scent of their own pups. Scent memories carry them back to those intense first weeks together.

Part of what the puppies perceive when watching other dogs' behavior is what those dogs are smelling or tasting. Dogs who watch another dog looking for food among several boxes greet the searcher by making contact with their snouts, sniffing them to see what the searcher has found. If they smell food, they go investigate the box where they observed the searcher before; if not, they don't bother.

੪੩

The WDC trainers are not, strictly speaking, training the *V* litter yet; they are still just exposing them to various noisy and new objects, in the spirit of generous socialization. As I watch them take every puppy through their paces, I see some of the other puppies, now tall and graceful compared to their puppy selves of just a month ago, doing something new: watching. This week, some pay attention to what the rest of the litter is doing. Vaz spots what Villa is up to and at first jumps and paws to try to get involved; eventually she backs herself up and just sits, taking in the scene. The flirt toy is deployed here by the trainers, too. Here, it is a long pole with ribbons of cloth attached to it. Jenny projects it toward Victoria, then dances it in front of her until she grabs and catches it. Victoria's interest is at first fleeting, but then she grabs it tenaciously. The next pup is surer of what to do after watching her sister. To Vega they shake a ring of a handful of keys and toss it; she bounds after it, grabs it like a small fluttering bird, play bows at it, then finally pins it with a paw and gnaws. *Gotcha!*

The trainers talk nonstop to their charges, but this week, less of it is baby talk. "Hello! Hello, sir!" Jenny coos at the boy, Vig. "Good morning! You're a bulldog. Hi! Hi!" Usually, Jenny says, she sees subtle differences among members of the litters she trains—one pup pulls, another wanders off, some are afraid of walking on a catwalk. Not with this litter, though. Sure, one is extra barky; another is bitey. But all are engaged with people and engage with the toys. In other words, they are perfect budding working dogs.

MARCH ❀ WEEK 8
Your Choice of Models

Suddenly it is upon us. Though this is just another drive up north to see Maize's puppies, I am uneasy. The puppies are eight weeks old, and it is nearly time for them to be adopted into permanent homes.

This means that I am now tasked with turning a different eye on them: a critical eye. By the end of next week, one of the puppies will be going home with us. Somehow I need to say yes to one and say no to ten others. How am I supposed to do that? And, moreover, why do I get to do that? Over the last few weeks I have felt increasingly on edge around Maize, knowing that soon people will come and take her puppies away one by one.

As I experience with every visit to an animal shelter, I want to take them all. (Hence I visit shelters rarely.) Well, not actually all. Eleven puppies are too many dimensions of puppyness. They are exhausting—the being jumped on, the freeing of sleeve and hair from teeth, the calling *pup pup puppy* into the wind. The looking out for them—subconsciously counting all the time, ensuring that there are still eleven, and that no one has found the pond or a hole in the fence.

Even if I harbor no fantasies of adopting all eleven, I hardly want to reject any. The very fact of making a selection feels clinical: treating them as objects rather than the living creatures they are. When you're buying a car, you can choose among the colors, choose the model and size; visit a litter of puppies, and something similar happens. I fight the urge to say that I would like a merle or a small one or one of the happy-go-lucky pups—to decide based on particular features. But the features are there for the seeing, and we tend to reason our way into a choice by weighing them. Rare features—a blue eye, a particularly dark or light coat—distinguish some puppies. A few have sprouted furnishings—those long hairs around the eyes and muzzle. I find a beard especially charming on a puppy. While I see each look as a tell about their personality—good or bad—Ogden and Ammon are very evenhanded about it: they like them all.

As I pull in I see one of Amy's dogs leaping back and forth over a high gate, freeing and then capturing herself. The calico cat is wandering among a small herd of sheep. From behind the house dogs appear and disappear, the larger ones followed dutifully by clusters of puppies. There is a new cadence to their activity upon my arrival: The huge thrill of a new! Person! Here! Then running-jumping excitement. Then they get interested in one another, in tumbling play; then they veer into different sports.

Their overall shape is still best described as roly-poly, with extra folds of skin around their faces and legs, but some are heading more toward gangly, others to pudgy. Their eyes have darkened from blue to a version of brown or hazel, though some retain a splinter of cerulean. Ears flop differently: perked upright, bowed deeply, cast half-mast. Only their tails are all cut from the same mold: each one half the length of the puppy, ending with a question mark curl.

I have noticed personality differences, too. Chaya is always a bit shy, less likely to be caught up in the contagion of puppies! running! after! something! we! don't! know! what! Cranberry, so vocal in the first weeks, is now thoughtful, sitting and observing (between gallops). There's the way one stops running to step gingerly around a patch of mud. Another bounds toward me when I call him, only to lose his train of thought midbound and race after a leaf floating by. A third runs with abandon to one of the big dogs, a border collie, and is roundly smacked by her; she slinks away. And today, one disappears.

Counting the puppies out in the Big Yard, we reach ten. The eleventh, Blue Camas, is inexplicably missing. We cross the broad field, looking at the fence with suspicion—does this bit under the deck push aside? Is that hole large enough for a small body to squeeze through? I worry that we have lost her, let all eight pounds of her wander out of human gaze and toward predatory animals and racing headlights outside the fence.

As we search, I remember when Pumpernickel, the first great dog love of my life, went missing. One night, returning home late, I found the front door wide open, light pouring out of the house into the darkness. The radio, which I had left on as audio company, still chattered on. But Pump was not in the house. Even as I panicked,

I began compiling a list of all the things I would need to do: walk and drive the routes we usually take, calling her name; visit the parks and beaches she knows; find a characteristic photo and put up posters with her face on light posts and telephone poles; call the local shelters and vets to ask about found dogs. Ultimately, I knew that these measures would be insufficient. She was, most likely, gone.

In fact, Pump did return that very night. I phoned friends who owned a local pet food store, asking them to come stay at the house while I began my futile walking and calling for her. On their arrival I saw Pump sitting calmly in the back seat. My friends had driven by their store en route to my home and saw her waiting there, patiently, for the store to open.

Even without knowing—or owning—Blue Camas, I got that same panic. The excitement of bringing a puppy home is streaked through with the realization of the responsibility for another life I am taking on.

We find Blue Camas. At some point she maneuvered indoors and found her way to her bed, where she promptly fell asleep. The relief of locating puppy eleven is matched by my surprise at how, in a moment of uncertainty, she raced toward the comfort of a crate with soft padding. Amy has begun putting them into crates at night, separating them from one another. She began by crating them in pairs, then gave each their own place to sleep at night, ignoring their protests. This crate training is meant to bridge them into the ultimate separation: into human homes, where there is no warm puppy pile to sleep in. By two weeks in, the puppies have adapted to this new reality—one more than the others.

More than choosing the "best" or my "favorite" pup, descriptions I could apply to any of them, I am struggling with knowing that in choosing one, I am saying a possibly permanent goodbye to the others. My choice feels extra loaded, too: I find myself believing that it is up to me to pick the right puppy for us—the one who can bear the attentions of a ten-year-old and the scrutiny of a dog scientist. Who can live in a city apartment or run around in the country. Who will be gentle with two older dogs and not eat the cat. Who will, in other words, fit fully into our family.

I look at each puppy, wondering, *Are you the one?*

ဆ

It has long been suggested that people have a soft spot for infants' features, such as their bulging cheeks and overlarge heads—features that prompt us to take care of them. But the appeal of the human baby might also explain our preference for certain nonhuman babies, even though most of them do not need our care. People prefer dogs with bigger eyes, smaller jowls, and a largish space between the eyes—all features that eight-week-old puppies have in spades. Indeed, it is the time that they are at their cutest. By asking undergraduates to rate the attractiveness of photos taken of Jack Russell, cane corso, and white shepherd puppies every week from their first to their twenty-eighth, one research study tried to identify puppies' "peak cuteness quotient." While all the puppies were seen as at least somewhat cute, the one-week-old sweet potatoes were rated as relatively uncute. Their superpower to cause spontaneous cooing behavior from humans increased weekly, until peaking at the impossibly cute form of eight-week-olds. Coincidentally this is also the time that most breeders and researchers think it is best to place a puppy in a human home. With their mothers' involvement waning and their bodies and brains maturing, they will leave their place of birth and be born anew.

At this age the puppies are also at a second transition point. Not only are they about to be thrust into another living situation, they are also going through a secondary socialization period—a developmental moment when they are maximally social and not yet too fearful of new things, people, sounds, and smells. But at this point, puppies' fearfulness is on the upswing and attraction to strangers is on the downswing. The startle response they began showing a few weeks earlier is spreading not just to actually startling things, but to novel things—things like a talking stuffed animal, a wobbly stairstep, or a spent balloon bopping across a lawn. If you have seen a dog crouch down warily, freeze in place, or tremble and bark or whine when approaching a puddle, that's the fear response showing its face. Tread gently, for the fear can overwhelm, or it can be approached gently and relieved.

Breeds differ in the time at which these fears might take hold: dogs bred to look more infant-like—such as Cavalier King Charles spaniels, who are bred to have small heads and big eyes—only begin to show fear responses at eight weeks. Dogs with longer noses and more wolfy features, like German shepherd dogs, startle to novel objects at five or six weeks—as the *V* litter and Maize's pups did. The spaniels' breeding actually slows their rate of development generally. This time of hypersensitivity to novel situations, which has long-term effects, might be part of why pet-store puppies at this age have more fear and anxiety than those raised properly by breeders or fosters: they are especially vulnerable, lacking the controlled socialization other puppies receive.

The flip side of the fear response is the development of attachment. If the world is scary, find a safe person and hold on tight. By this age puppies show just the kind of behavior we see in young children who have formed a secure attachment to an adult: If exposed to a new place or person, then separated from their mother, the pups become distressed. They try to get back to her; they cry. But they are flexible, and brought into a family of humans, they redirect that attention and bond toward one of us.

All puppies are still approaching new people and dogs with confidence and a wagging tail—and that is why researchers believe this is the best time to place a pup into a human home. Mom has completed weaning and is probably highly irritated with her pups; they are getting more aggressive in their play with one another. They are cognitively quite advanced from their abilities two months ago. They are now pretty good at controlling their impulses, stopping, say, from lunging at a large transparent plastic canister if they can see a tempting piece of food inside it. Instead, most pups can figure out to search around the canister for the opening. Their memory span is getting longer, and they no longer have forgotten completely about the toy you took from their mouths and hid behind your back; thirty seconds later they may look at you expectantly or just go find it themselves. In short, they are ready to leave the nest.

Everyone has a tale of finding their dog, and most have an air of inevitability: "When we saw her, we just knew she was the one." Scientists have looked at puppy selection, too. I know my own choice is based on emotion as much as knowledge. I am drawn to certain dogs by how they look, for the behaviors they show. I trace my choice of Pumpernickel to her sitting on my sneakered feet, looking up at my face; of Finnegan for the way he leaned against me when we met; of Upton for his winning tail thump on seeing me approach his cage. Certainly, how a dog is acting at the moment is relevant—a puppy who uses barking to communicate now is likely to continue to bark in the future; a dog who shies away from people at eight weeks will have more trouble overcoming that fear later. Research backs me up: in one study, dogs who lie down by a potential adopter were fourteen times more likely to be adopted than those who did not; dogs who did not respond to a request to play were the least likely to be adopted. Given that people spend approximately eight minutes with a dog before deciding whether to adopt them or not, the process is not entirely rational.

It turns out that the puppies are as irrational as we are. Puppies are not in a position to choose their people, but they can and do make choices—if sometimes odd ones. Researchers giving eight-week-old puppies choices between two quantities of food—one piece of kibble or four—found that they chose a single piece just as often as they took more. Adult dogs, as all people who live with dogs know, do not make this mistake. They may be better at counting; they may be better at maximizing their choices—or simply better at seeing when there is a choice to be made.

Most likely, two-month-old puppies simply do not yet realize that they exist in a world of choices, of which they can select some options and discard others. They will come to realize it in time. Just not yet.

MARCH ❧ WEEK 9
Calm Before the Storm

We have entered preparation mode. We need to get the stuff, learn the training, roll up our sleeves, brace ourselves. Ever the scientist, I regale Ammon and Ogden with puppy facts, with reminders of how puppies learn, with how we should behave. They listen and nod, and then do their own thing: Ammon constructs a small fenced area by the house for early-morning outings; Ogden simply lies on the couch, staring at the ceiling, grinning mightily.

Our first joint action is deciding on a name. While all the puppies have been provisionally named, we will rename the one who is coming home with us. To give a puppy a name is to begin their life with us—to start them on the track of being part of our family. We take long walks with the dogs, lobbing suggestions to each other, considering some, rejecting others out of hand.

On the evening before we drive to pick up the puppy, we sit down on the floor to decide. We have eighteen candidates. We have animal names (Otter), weather phenomena (Zephyr), old-fashioned human names (Eudora, Sigrid, Steig), even punctuation (Tilde). Beginning with our list of eighteen, each of us chooses six top names and can eliminate one. Then we repeat with the remaining names, choosing five, eliminating one, and so on.

Eudora, never a great candidate, disappears quickly. Down go *Sid* and *Sigrid*. When we are down to two apiece, we are granted the right to bring one of our eliminated favorites back into the game. Ogden brings back *Squall*, which turns out to be the name of a pet in a book he is reading; Ammon resuscitates *Em Dash*, a joining punctuation, which felt like a way to add a third dog to a two-dog family.

Our final round has *Em Dash*, *Squall*, and *Quid*—another of Ogden's suggestions. We have one last vote apiece. Ammon and I converge on a name, and *Em Dash* wins. The moment of the choice, I look at them both with anticipation: Did we just begin to meet our puppy? We agree to sleep on it.

In the morning we list the pros and cons of each name and bring back any names that might have haunted our dreams. This is a word we are going to be saying thousands of times, I remind us—maybe a thousand times in the first week alone. We ought to make it something we are happy to say out loud. A lot. On this reckoning *Quid* wins—with *Quiddity* as the full name. The word means the essence of a thing: a thing's thingness. The common element of all the puppies is how perfectly puppy they all are. This time, we all nod in agreement. It's *Quid*.

The click of the name into place makes it real: a puppy named Quid is about to come home. A name feels like the first step in making her a good, happy dog—outlining the kind of dog she can be. At the same time, I know that the notion that by naming a dog we somehow command who they will be is impossible. Puppies are a force of nature, like thunderstorms, uncontrollable, only observable from a safe (or unsafe) distance. I know this—but I need to put away this understanding for just long enough to bring the puppy home.

Now we just need to get her. Quid does not even know we're coming.

In fact, we do not get a choice of eleven. As their caretaker, Amy was charged with trying to match puppy to person. In the last week or two, she has predetermined which puppy she thinks would fit with our family, based on the personalities she's seen blossoming and the potential adopters clamoring at her door. She offered us a few candidates, then let us choose among them. I suggest one to my family—the female, given the strong male energy currently in our home—and they agree enthusiastically. Still, I want to think about it one more night, to be sure. Finnegan, listening to us talking, looks at me with mournful eyes; I glance at Upton, who lifts his front leg for a consoling chest rub.

On my final visit I looked at each of the puppies and realized how little prepared I was to decide against one. I wondered if I could make the right choice by just typing rapidly and seeing what came out—by sending my subconscious mind into my fingers before my conscious brain interfered. It didn't work. I only ended up with this on my screen:

> i went o see both of them. well, i got 11. they alllooked
> good. nnn cn

PART 2

SECOND BIRTH

APRIL ❋ WEEK 10
Arrival of the Storm

We've got her.

Before dawn on an overcast morning, my mind wakes me up with a string of thoughts—*Oh, we need a sling for carrying her while we walk the dogs; do we have another water bowl? What about nail trimmers?* I look over at the dogs on the bed. Finn's feet are padding through a dream; Upton yawns lazily. They don't know what is about to happen.

Because of the pandemic, we haven't gotten to a store—nor have store deliveries come to us—so we don't have a puppy gate. Instead, we find an old privacy screen that belonged to my grandmother. She used to dress behind it; it is dotted with colorful mirrored spangles. She would be surprised to see it put to use to create two walls lining a puppy-safe space in the living room.

By noon we are home with a puppy. Three hours later and she is sleeping on a soft bed in a soft-sided carrier, like a pro. So much has happened in just three hours. I look at her and wonder how she is processing this entire series of events: she has gone from being among all her siblings, to her first car ride, to wearing a harness and leash, to meeting two big dogs, a *cat!*, an entirely new space with smaller spaces within it, balls filled with kibble, toys filled with treats.

Several hours ago she was lying under a tent on the other side of a fence, flanked by eight of her siblings, when we pulled into Amy's driveway. Two puppies, Persimmons and Chaya, were already off to their new homes. Maize was inside, out of sight.

All the pups rise as we approach, disentangling themselves from one another. Wild Ramps is first at the fence to greet us; various noses and tongues and claws touch my hand through the chain link. Amy steps out of the house, looking cheery. She neatly picks up Wild Ramps and heads into the house. Five minutes later, they return, Wild Ramps in a towel, a bath having transformed her into a wee mouse. Amy is still rubbing her dry as she hands her to me. She is dense and warm and delivers impressively soft licks to my face. I hand her to Ogden, who can hardly contain himself. For the first time, we meet Quiddity.

Amy takes a photo of Quid and me, pressing the button just as the puppy's tongue reaches my face. Later I will see photos of the other families who arrived today. The puppies are dispersing to New Jersey, upstate New York, Rhode Island, Massachusetts. There is a poignancy to seeing the puppies, still more part of the litter than they are their own persons, going off into their separate lives.

In the back seat of the car, we plop Quiddity in a cat bed in the center seat; she is cat-size and can easily curl her body into a comma. Ogden and I sit on either side of her. She is stuffed-animal cute, mostly black with perfectly placed drops of paint: two round rust-colored eyebrows; the tip of her snout, tail, and each of her paws dipped in white. Her eyes are small and searching; her ears,

The moment that Quid joined our family

large and soft, folded in the middle under their own weight. White whiskers ring her muzzle, and the tiniest streak of pink is visible on her lips. She is trembling but calmly searches the space with her eyes and nose. It is a lot to take in. Bath (new), car (new), new people. Smells of car (new), moving car (new). She takes turns sitting on the bed and moving between us. I slip a harness on her without her noticing, though later she looks suspiciously at this thing she has found around her midriff (harness: new). Although it is new as well, quite soon she is settled on Ogden's lap, her head becomingly on his knee. New but perfect. Halfway through the drive home I take over driving so Ammon can meet her in the back seat, but it is too late: she has already committed to Ogden's lap for the ride.

At home I run inside to get the dogs. "Something very exciting!" I tell them, bringing them to the small fenced-in area behind the house for the puppy. The puppy comes into view, on leash, led by Ogden. She is sniffing and peeing and agreeably following, wagging heartily. I could not have predicted what they would do on meeting. The dogs are interested but calm; they give her a perfunctory sniff and then go on their way, as though they meet a new puppy by their house every day. Quid, though, is quite alarmed at the sight of these dogs and immediately tucks her tail between her legs. She looks perfectly miserable. Though she has been around Big Dogs for her entire life, these are New Big Dogs—about the twentieth new thing in the last hour—and she ducks her head into the crook of Ammon's arm. Ogden skips around the enclosure with the dogs, calling her name a hundred times, giggling with pleasure.

As with just about everything thus far, though, she just needs a little time: even as we pause, deciding what to do, she becomes bolder. As Ammon puts her down on the ground, she musters the courage to reach her nose out toward the dogs from the safety of his feet, stretching as far as she can without moving her rump.

It is raining lightly, so we head for New Thing number twenty-one: inside. She enters this unknown space with hesitation. We sit down with her as the cat rises to greet us. Edsel gives a fiery look, new to this occasion, and stalks over to examine this alien creature. Their colors—black, brown, white—are identical, only painted differently. They do not seem to appreciate this commonality, and the puppy turns her head away as the cat sneezes and prances off.

While we are ready to sit still for a bit, the puppy is just getting started. So we begin some gentle training, giving her a treat if she looks at us or if she sits down. She is either ravenous or a good learner, for in ten minutes she has received three dozen treats. Ogden instructs us all on the routine he has learned: show her a handful of treats, hold that hand by your belly button, and expect that the puppy will jump. When the puppy jumps, ignore her. When she finally sits and looks at you, quickly crouch a bit and place a small reward in her mouth. The Ogden-Quid team demonstrate ably, as though they have been practicing for months.

With a puppy this young the strategy of "waiting until she does a behavior that you like and then rewarding her for it" works beautifully—because she is always trying out new behaviors. Her life involves moving between twelve behaviors in ten seconds, and it is just up to us to catch the ones we like as they flit by. She may be biting my hand now, but the next moment she is carrying a rope toy proudly and then running after a moth wandering by. There is no idling for puppies: they are chasing the next moment before it happens.

Two hours pass, and Ogden remembers that it is time to take her outside to pee again. Puppies cannot be expected to hold their bladders, or even know that they are not holding their bladders, so by taking her out every two hours, we let her be that puppy without ruining the carpets. So we head to the penned area where she first met the dogs.

She seems quite uncertain what is to happen there. A ladder lies on the ground, and she does some fine footwork through the rungs; she mouths some inedibles—a rock, an acorn; she zoomies around the perimeter. A crow caws, and she stops, gazing out beyond the fence, then tries to jump through the fence. But she does not pee, so we head back inside.

The pace of our day becomes inside, outside, inside; hesitation, action, hesitation. And, finally, epic naps. As the sun sets, she begins tearing around the house madly, as though trying to outrun her own tail. She runs until she conks out, literally on her feet.

She naps for two and a half hours. We were tiptoeing around the house but now are making normal amounts of noise; nothing rouses her. When the dogs finish dinner, they come and poke their noses over the wall to her corner of the living room, sniffing. The cat, who has been running around chasing the sounds of squirrels on the roof, suddenly becomes very suspicious of who is on the soft bed in the corner of the room and observes from a safe distance until she can go in and check her out. I am waiting for the day when they curl up together, but it is not today.

The day is long, and we take Quid out and in a dozen times, gently trying to show her how the leash is attached to both her and us. She fails to see the connection, pulling ahead, across, between our legs in comically intricate fashion. I start calling her *the puppy*, as contrasted with *the dogs*, as she seems like an entirely different *species*.

For one thing, she is a light bulb burning bright. When she is on, you can't not notice her: she is chewing, running, peeing, scratching, whining—doing. With her addition, the air inside the house is charged, full of potential energy.

At night she falls asleep in a canvas crate, in her dressing-screen-walled room in a new home, in a new city, without any of her siblings. We all sneak into our beds and whisper memories of the many things that have happened that day. Several hours into the night, I hear some whining. I would say it was a yodel, almost a bark, then many yodels—not something I would like to hear in the middle of the night. Oh, wait . . . it *is* the middle of the night . . .

I am up late, in the dressing-screen-walled room in my home, with a new puppy. Ammon promises to take over the early-morning shift.

The rest of the week is a blur of this new creature in our home every hour of every day. She bites the cat in the face and bothers the dogs, who have taken, rightfully, to just turning away in disdain. Upton has a new growl, and Finn is grumpy all the time. Quid's mouth has been on most surfaces in the home, including the couch, the chair, the table, and grandmother's screen. She has gnawed on dog toys but also fingers, sticks, pencils, books, the wall, and the cat's ears. At the same time, she is impossibly cute. It is satisfying to pick up a small, warm bundle of puppy. Along the length of her nose, a line of hairs stands erect, a mohawk of the nose: we call it her *nohawk*. When she is uncertain she pulls her ears back against her head, morphing into a little fox mouse.

We take her for several short runs in nearby parks: when she is off the leash, she is a steam engine, barreling away. She attends, and dozes through, her first Zoom meeting. She eats a stalk of broccoli. She tries to leap up the single step from the yard to the deck, as tall as she is. She makes it. She pees outside. And inside. And going from inside to outside. She does not sleep through the night.

She is a baby, but she appears more like an adult fully packed into a small dog's body. She does not know what matters (to us), what is happening next (to her), what to expect and do. We didn't just adopt a dog; we took on her education into everything human.

🦴

Bookstore shelves sag under the weight of instructional books for this key moment when a new dog enters the house for the first time. The best of them stress that it's not going to be a part-time gig: "Make time for exercise and fun activities and . . . gentle activity . . . and establish . . . a schedule for eating, toileting and event/crate time and play . . . plenty of naps . . . nail trimming, baths, vet/groomer visits," one trainer advises. The list of "vital supplies" you must have for your puppy has gotten ever longer over the years. It now likely includes at least the following: crate, dog bed, baby gates for every opening, a variety of toys, different puppy foods, plentiful treats, treat bag, leash, collar, dog brush, nail trimmers, toothbrush . . . more things than one packs for sleepaway camp. New dog people dutifully shop their way to being prepared, since these books are the only operating manuals provided on how to navigate this new situation.

This advice is not wrong. But while a checklist can be helpful, what is unstated in each of those books is the struggle that so many people have with their new pups. The struggle is real. And it is due to the collision of dog and human worlds that is apparent from the first hours of bringing home a new dog. Especially for those who have never lived with dogs, the experience can be shocking. This might account for the number of people who return their dogs to the shelter or breeder within months of acquiring them, usually for reasons of being a dog: barking, being excitable, not knowing where to pee, damaging the house, difficulty making friends with other pets, not understanding the rules of the house. All are called "misbehavior" on the intake forms, but what they are is "normal puppy behavior."

Dogs don't know how to live in our homes, don't respect the pronouns we put on items—*that's* my *bed*—don't have a clue about the identities we give to objects: *That's a shoe, not a chew toy!* Despite the social appearance of dogs as (more or less) cooperatively walking alongside their people in public, sitting peaceably at our feet at sidewalk restaurants, taking their seat in our cars (nose peeking out the window), dogs don't naturally come to these behaviors. Walking with us is awkward: we are not at the dog's pace. Dogs are sprinters, not long-distance walkers. Moreover, they don't want to go in a straight line, keeping an even gait. They zigzag, stop and sniff, run off to chase unseen moving creatures in the grass. They turn around, go sideways, stop entirely. They wait for other dogs; they pull for other dogs. They smell a spot on the ground intently for minutes. Sitting with us is agreeable enough—unless there is anything at all happening nearby, in which case they must bark, lunge, investigate, jump, or retreat. Cars are doubly strange places to occupy: the first experience most dogs will have of their bodies moving at high speeds without their control, a world of smells racing by outside the window.

Research into dog behavior might give the impression that they are born ready to live in a human world. Dogs do have a natural interest in people. From the very first weeks that they can see, they look at any available people; they approach people; they lick at people, run with people, and as every puppy in Maize's litter has done, occupy any available human laps. They follow our gaze and pointing, as we have seen. This is a good start. But following a point is a far cry from understanding the human rules of social interaction, how to behave at home, and how to behave outside with new people and dogs.

Imagine needing to learn not just how to be a dog but how to be a dog among humans. It is no wonder that the first weeks of life with a puppy are challenging. While we spend our lives trying to learn how to be good humans, we now are tasked with teaching another species how to do so, too.

To add to the species divide, by the time a puppy is old enough to leave her mom and come live with us, she is the developmental equivalent of a preteen. She is also at the tail end of her socialization period, learning about the world. All the exposures to dogs, cats, music, cars, people, and the occasional low-flying helicopter that she experienced along with her litter need to continue. Until she is twelve to fourteen weeks old, she is especially receptive to new things. But even after that age socialization needs to be kept up, or those "misbehaviors" are likely to be a dog's response to something new later in their life. In our own puppy's case, her world just expanded, whether she was ready for it or not, to include an already complete family of three species.

How that tween will behave depends on us more than we would like to think. Oh, sure, some of it arises from the equipment she comes with—the keen nose, the alert ears, the flexibility to see people as family. The brain she has, the body she wears, her parents' genes. Her way of acting on the world—with a mouth, not a hand; in close proximity, not at human-handshake distance. But in these several critical weeks of early development, she wields those tools to engage with the environment she is exposed to. They help her organize what she hears, feels, sees, and smells. So much of what we see her doing in her first week in a new home is starting that project. We are witnessing the unity of mind and body as she takes in this bright new world and learns to act in it. The world becomes divided into things that she can engage with and those she can't; friendly and unfriendly, prey and predator, stranger and family. She is forming categories. The more we can help her see that, to us, fingers are not "things that can be mouthed," while sticks may be, the better equipped she will be among people.

We are so completely familiar with our worlds, especially inside our home, that we can forget that this new creature will experience it differently. It is not a dog bed to her; it is something soft, marked by its proximity to (or distance from) other people and dogs, maybe smelling of a dog who used it before. Exploration by mouth happens at mouth level, so the book and the dog toy on the floor get the same treatment.

We're bringing home a dog. We all think we are doing something as simple as that phrase: just adding them to our already-intact home. The great surprise is that they change our home. As soon as she crossed the threshold into our house, Quid changed the space inside. She changed how we use the spaces, how we think of the furniture. People seats become puppy seats. Table legs and bookcases are chew toys. More often than not we all wind up on the floor, crammed into the Quid-designated space, while the rest of the furniture huddles together, recovering from the inexhaustible puppy.

Nicknames used with the puppy in her first week with us:

QUID

QUIDQUID

QUIDDLE

QUIDNUNC (when she's acting
pleasingly naughty)

QUIDSOME

Q

BEASTIE

GREMLIN

EARS (Finn is Nose;
Upton is Mouth.)

PUPPY-DO

PUPPER

PEST

PEANUT

PEANUT SAUCE

LITTLE ONE

APRIL ❀ WEEK 11
(Im)perfect Puppy

It's 3:15 in the morning. Quiddity is howling. She is doing her best coyote impression in our living room to an audience of one. It is her third performance this night. Somehow I am the only one awakened. I stay perfectly still, willing her voice still. If she quiets for even a minute, I will go and lie down by her crate, hoping some company will calm her. That is what one of us has done every night for the last several nights. I am sleep-deprived and grumpy.

She does not stop, and eventually I go down anyway, grumbling as I go. I might have said "I hate her" under my breath. At night all my concerns are amplified, as though they feed off darkness: I worry that we have made a mistake. She is the wrong dog, the wrong breed of dog. She is too demanding. I don't like having to be on top of everything, anticipating the next need to pee or object that will be chewed. I am worried about the stress she is placing on the dogs: Finn is constantly sending me accusatory glances; I feel sure that he has gotten new gray hairs on his muzzle. Upton has stopped playing with us altogether and often just up and leaves a room when we enter (puppy at our heels). She is overneedy and underfoot. I lack the energy required to maintain the encouraging, enthusiastic tone of voice needed to get her attention, to egg her on to climb that step, to follow me, to stay off, down, there. I am needed, and I do not want to be needed. I churn with irritation and impatience.

Even worse, I am impatient with my impatience. I know better. *Be patient* is the first thing I say to people who come to me for advice about their new puppy. "This too shall pass," I say, looking at my calm, professional dogs, who are models of restraint and charm. And it does pass—and, if they hold tight, they get through early puppyhood before they know it and form the bond they thought they were signing up for. My puppy regrets, even my moments of aversion, are expected. Yet in those moments they are real.

I know the puppy's cries are communication. She is alone. She is crying because she is alone. I know how to fix it, but there are only so many dogs who can fit on our bed. We introduced her to a lovely soft crate, filled with soft bedding, just as she had had at Amy's house. At the start of the night, she toddles in peaceably. In the middle of the night, she wants to be anywhere else. In my sleepiness I turn the concern into "Will this be her personality for-ever?" My answer is yes; my conclusion is "We made a mistake."

In the morning Ammon reminds me that, several weeks into living with Finn, I told him, "You know, he's very cute, but I just don't think I'll fall in love with him." And we both remember crying with anxiety after adopting Upton, who was untrained in leashes or relaxation. Now I look at disgruntled, sweet, ever-earnest Finn and the goofy, good-natured Upton and love them so much.

Ammon takes the puppy to his office for the day while I work. He reports that she sleeps happily at his feet. Well, no wonder, she was up all night.

ဒၧ

Spring is reluctant to arrive this year; a late snowstorm causes the daffodils to hang their heads. Quiddity stands in the doorway, looking out at the snow with hesitation. Then she throws herself outside and headlong into it.

Her general-purpose exuberance can be contagious, even when I am feeling sleepy and frosty toward her. I find myself grinning widely later when, snow-tired, she plops onto my lap. Her nohawk is blossoming nicely and now is matched by great tufts of hair growing out on either side of her chin. Feathering is sprouting on the backs of her legs, extrending outward, like the grasses pushing up through the cold earth. Her ears are growing faster than the rest of her tiny head: giant triangular rockets aimed straight at the moon. But I soften most when she pulls them back and flat against her head. One morning we find that her ears have dropped, folding in half to flop when she trots along. It is cute but disconcerting. Tomorrow, will her tail start shortening?

After three weeks of mostly ignoring her, the dogs suddenly, after dinner, turn to look at Quid in a new way: as a possible play-mate. She is beyond excited, her tail wagging her entire body. Upton looks gigantic, comically so, next to her. Given her outsize presence, it is a shock to see how little she is among the dogs. He stays mostly lying on the ground, letting her hop back and forth over him, gently pursuing her with a wide-open mouth. Finn tag teams, nibbling her flank as though eating corn on the cob. Quid pulls out all her play moves. She rolls over, nips and tucks, licks each dog's mouth, and somersaults repeatedly, sometimes to hide under my feet or the couch. But she keeps coming out. A five-minute all-out session turns into hours of off-and-on play. I am cheered to see the dogs acknowledge her positively. Their mutual game makes it seem as though they have been plotting the best way to deal with this new creature.

Soon, every night after dinner, the red carpet in the center of the living room turns into a kind of stage for dog play. Quid snuffles as she bites the folds of skin on Upton: his jowls, the loose skin around his neck. A few times she has gotten her head in his mouth, some-how, and he gags as she holds on to his tongue. Half the time he seems to love it, his tail curving over his back with pleasure, his mouth whale-trawling through the air. Then he growls severely. Quid knows what that means. He is communicating simply and effectively, and she lies down, ears pressed flat against her head.

Unlike Upton, I need to work at communicating with Quid. She picks things up with surprising ease when she knows we are talking to her. "Why don't we all get puppies at this young age?" I wonder aloud. Yesterday she learned to stop what she is doing and look at me when I call her. Frankly, this is better than what our dogs, with whom we have lived for a dozen years, will do. She steps into her harness with the encouragement of a few of the tini-est pieces of kibble. Amazingly she is now peeing outside in the same place, after we did nothing but bring her there.

We take her to a nearby pathway fenced on both sides to practice her "recall," coming when called. I drop her leash and run away from her; she chases me happily—and quickly catches up, looking at me to see what's next. Two hundred yards back, Ammon and Ogden turn and run in the other direction, then call her name. She tears toward them, a furry bullet. And then after the small celebration for catching them, I call her back to me—and then they to them, and on and on.

I see that she *is* trainable. And she is busily training us, too. Ogden starts a game of chase by rolling a ball across the room for her. As she picks it up and brings it back, he squeaks another and rolls it, causing her to drop the first one and chase the second. Or, from her perspective, she drops a ball to cause him to roll the second so she can chase it. She is wagging, and Ogden is laughing. She has trained us to take her outside with a particular searching look, performed dramatically on the first stair of the staircase leading to our bedroom. It took us only one instance of her peeing on a thick-pile carpet before we learned the meaning of that look.

The next week is all water as spring turns south. We awaken to rain and violent winds, and Quid trembles as we open the door. She refuses to go out but gazes with great interest at the dogs, who survive the attacking air and the wet ground. She rallies for breakfast and in her enthusiasm steps completely into her bowl of water. She pulls out her feet with what can only be described as a look of horror—followed by a reproachful look at me, the person clearly responsible for all this.

The following day we bundle everyone into the car to go for a longer walk, releasing some of the energy stored up yesterday. We all step cautiously out onto a pier projected over a pond; the dogs peek over the side at actual frogs sitting on actual lily pads. Quid does not step cautiously: she reaches for one of the frogs, and she, the frog, and the lily pad all go under.

I have never lived with a dog who has not fallen into a body of water once. Nor have I lived with a dog who has fallen in a second time. Quid is determined to defy this trend. Later in the week we visit a friend with an in-ground pool, surrounded by a glorious meadow for running in—which Ogden and Quid are. Fifteen seconds after our friend says "Don't let her fall into the pool," she . . . slips into the pool.

Each time, I find myself thinking two thoughts at once: *Oh no!* (followed by my racing to the edge of the body of water) and *Dog paddle is well named* (as her front paws ably churn the water in front of her, keeping her head above the surface). She is surprisingly good at it, given that these are her first times in bodies of water. I scoop her into my arms, reining in her scrabbling claws. She is more saturated than it feels possible. Her fur is doused; her ears droop. Her tail is leaden. On land and on her feet again, she rolls frantically in the grasses, then takes off, as though she can outrun the sensation of her body. Later, when she is fully dried, her fur is extra scruffy; even her scruff has scruff.

Back at home, a dryish puppy at my feet, the cat is staring me down. Quid has overcome her initial concern and is now treating Edsel as another dog, a playmate. She assumes it is perfectly okay to, say, bite the cat's face. And, when Edsel hisses and swats at her, to bark and chase her under the couch. Quid meets and remeets the cat a dozen times a day, each time seeming to be as excited as the first time. We followed an episode of cat chasing with a session of rewarding Quid with food for sitting and looking at me, doing nothing cat directed when the cat is nearby. Edsel looks irked but sticks around.

One reason the cat's around is that the arrival of Quid has brought new sleeping arrangements and eating opportunities. Finn has perked up considerably since we suddenly always carry smelly dog treats on our walks. Edsel, too, comes in at dinnertime and demonstrates her command of food puzzle balls. Quid watches her and tries to dart in when the food topples out, but Edsel gobbles it up—eating quite a bit faster than she consumes her own dinner.

By now the small dog bed we bought for Quid is usually occupied by Edsel. Quid tries to fit in there with her, and Edsel discourages her in no uncertain terms, hissing with a seriousness that is hard to mistake. I have never seen Edsel's whiskers so flared: a bearded dragon's worth. They are each communicating well, but not with their audience in mind. Edsel cannot translate the play bow; Quid misinterprets the swat. In what looks to me like a gesture of peace, Edsel approaches a resting Quid and licks her right on the nose. Quid growls, and Edsel saunters off. Their miscommunications are not so unlike our own, as we struggle with telling Quid what we need or with giving her what she seems to. I gaze at Edsel with what I hope she reads as a shared sense of struggle.

But I sympathize with the puppy, too. She has lost her puppy companions—the bodies, matching hers, that show her where to go, what to do, whom to bite, what to pick up, when to run, when to rest. That has all disappeared in a flash. So Edsel looks like a good candidate for such camaraderie, perhaps. Both dogs have by now indulged Quid's habit of lying in the crook of their bodies: she is a body-crook locator. And she has made the move to nap with her head fully resting on Upton—Upton willing—or on one of our feet or on a stuffed toy. She is piling with the only pileable items available.

When I remember this, we bring her sleeping crate into Ogden's bedroom, setting it by his bed. If not on a body, near one. We visit her before bed ourselves and hear her suckling in her sleep. A full moon, bright, keeps me up listening for the slightest yowl. The next morning I write in my notebook, in all caps: *SLEEPS THROUGH THE NIGHT!*

Maybe I don't hate her. But I don't love her. Yet.

🦴

The television personality Cesar Millan wrote a book titled *How to Raise the Perfect Dog*. The skillful trainer Dr. Sophia Yin wrote *Perfect Puppy in 7 Days*. I find the language of perfection in regard to puppies to be both hilarious and tragic. The hilarity is that, of course, they are perfect straightaway. They are soft bundles of pleasure who let you pet them and who gaze into your eyes! Perfect! The tragedy is the notion that the goal of training should be perfect behavior or perfect enactment of several commands. One of the pleasures of dogs is that they are full of messy behaviors: this is why we do not adopt robots.

I wish there were training books for new dog people entitled *Perfect Person in 7 Days*. All you need to do to be a perfect person for your dog is to keep an open mind about who our dogs are and how they should be acting in this new environment. Oh, and to learn to be consistent in how you talk to dogs—and to learn how they are talking to us.

We are working on that curriculum at home. For us, learning Quid's signs—the way she is talking already—involves an intensive lesson in observation. We are watching her constantly, trying to see what look precedes what action, what she notices, and what she responds to. And one must not arrive with preconceptions.

Four hours into living with Quid, we were already describing her personality: who she was, why she was acting the way she was. Ninety minutes of that time, she was asleep. This is typically human of us. But people don't enter into human relationships thinking we know everything about another person. We get to know people by seeing what they do and listening to what they say. With dogs, somehow, we work backward: we talk about how and who our dogs are from the moment we meet them. It would be the rare dog person who does not make any claims about what their new dog wants, desires, or even thinks within a week of knowing them. We speak for our dogs, talking about what they like and dislike, and explain their behavior as caused by fears, thoughts, and passions.

Watching our own dogs deal with the newcomer is a master class in attending and communicating. Visit a dog park in any city and you will see rules for dogness being followed, flouted, and enforced—

until the dog people step in and mess things up. Upton's growl at Quid was his way of telling her that she had stepped over the line; her response was immediate and deflected any further upset.

This is not to say that a person, too, should growl—or yell or shout—at a puppy when she does something undesired. Upton's growl works because that growl means something specific—and is perfectly timed. To a puppy our yelling can mean many things and may or may not happen when the unhappy-making action did, leaving a puppy thinking that whatever they just did (like coming over to you when you called) prompted the yelling. As important, because we are the ones who are controlling where the puppy can be, can sit, can eat, can pee, can sleep, and how and when they are allowed to do perfectly natural dog behaviors like biting and running, we as yellers are also in quite a different position toward the puppy than dogs as growlers.

For pups it is a tricky business transitioning from living among dogs—in a society maintained by dog rules, communicated by dogs to dogs—to living among people. Part of the Perfect Person curriculum is imagining what that might be like for them: translating what we want to what they can hear, and translating what they are doing to what they mean. It is remembering what Quid's first weeks were like—the close contact and puppy pile that she grew up in—in designing a space at our home where she can thrive.

And it is remembering that a puppy's enthusiasm takes shape as energy—sound energy. As soon as the puppy is projected into our world, they begin making noises. We might call those noises whimpers or cries, but they are all just early expressions of the energy that is bottled in them. We have had some glimpses of this in Quid's nighttime noisemaking. The reason is simple: whines and yelps worked to get her mother's attention; now they are transforming into other vocalizations that mean more or less the same thing. The bark heard round the city—the "alone" bark, high in pitch and frequency—evolves straight out of those early pup squeaks.

What all the perfect-puppy books are selling really has nothing to do with perfection: it has to do with training a dog to be more like what we, in today's culture, assume dogs should be like.

Happily, the method of training currently in vogue is based on positive reinforcement. What all training is intended to do is to get dogs to learn things of value to us—and to learn which of their behaviors we approve of and which we do not. This form of learning is called operant conditioning and is based on the notion that dogs and people and everyone else learn effectively by connecting what we do to the consequences of what we do. As we wander around the world behaving, we find that certain actions (operations) are followed by delightful consequences, others by nasty ones. Whether we do that action again, or don't, depends on whether the result was something we wanted. Training, then, is creating a context in which a dog can naturally learn (condition) these associations.

Positive-reinforcement training is the good guy of learning. I get to realize that something I do, intentional or not, leads to something super: a reinforcement or reward. Imagine that I come across a vending machine with cookies inside and levers on the outside. I pull a lever and a cookie is released where I can take it.

I quickly learn that lever pulling is an excellent way to get cookies. That is positive reinforcement. I like cookies. I will doubtless try that lever again.

That is simple enough. To train a dog this way, you need to wait until they do a behavior you like, though. You need to catch them in the act so that you can deliver a perfectly timed reward for that specific behavior. Every person you see congratulating their puppy for peeing on a patch of grass outside is doing this form of training.

Positive reinforcement is not the only form of operant conditioning, though. If, instead of getting a cookie when I pull a lever, I get a shock, you can be sure I will be reluctant to do it again. That is called positive punishment: *positive* because something new happened—the shock—and *punishment* because it was, well, shocking, and done to reduce my rate of lever pulling.

Positive punishment, though it sounds like something beneficial, is what most people mean when they say *punishment*: spanking, yelling, hitting. It is not a positive feeling, but it indicates an addition (plus, thus *positive*) of something to the dog's world. There is also a method called negative punishment, which is taking away (minus, thus *negative*) something that is liked. If I am touching all the levers, getting all the cookies, and you don't want me to, then you rig the machines so they no longer give cookies. I will probably stop pulling the levers (eventually).

Finally there is negative reinforcement learning, in which you increase the rate of a behavior by taking away something bad. If the cookie machine is buzzing loudly and I can fix it by banging on its side, I have learned by negative reinforcement that machine banging miraculously makes things better. This form of learning is used quite a bit in horse training: by pulling on the reins to try to get a horse to slow down, the horse may learn that if they slow when they feel this unpleasant pressure on their face, the pressure will stop (if the rein pulling is done right).

We—and dogs—learn from all these methods in our ordinary lives. Stick your finger in a bottle and get it stuck, and you are less likely to do that again (positive punishment). Scream—or bark—and everyone comes running over to you to see what you need, and you are more likely to do that again (positive reinforcement). A dog who is able to chew through their crate to escape confinement becomes a crate chewer (negative reinforcement); one who finds that you put the tennis ball away when they bring it to you becomes less likely to bring it to you (negative punishment).

The great debate among trainers and in psychology concerns which is the most effective learning method. In terms of longevity of learning, training via positive reinforcement wins. Positive punishment—yelling "No!" at a puppy—can be effective in stopping a behavior, but it comes with lots of side effects: the punishment needs to be timed perfectly or it is unclear what behavior to stop; it can lead to the recipient becoming generally fearful, angry, or aggressive; and it gives no clue to what behavior would be good instead. Thus it can lead to learned helplessness, or feeling unable to act at all.

Learning via the good guy means that if your puppy is barking in another room in the middle of the night (for example), you do not go in there and yell at them. Instead, when they are quiet, you sneak in and reward them with your presence. There, the behavior being reinforced is actually *not barking*. Since it can take some serious patience to wait until *not barking* occurs, the positive-punishment move—yelling—is a common mistake. No one feels better after that—and the pup may still bark.

While positive-reinforcement training is popular now, it is not the only form of training used by dog trainers. In fact, negative punishment—ignoring a dog doing something you dislike—is quite often used with it. It is fairly harmless. But if a trainer recommends an e-collar, which delivers a shock or stimulation, that is classic positive punishment. In the past, methods using this form of punishment were much more common. Nineteenth- and early twentieth-century training manuals were likely to use the word *correction* and to talk about "cuffs on the nose" as part of the tool kit of the trainer. It was classic positive punishment, through and through.

I think good training is mispitched: it should be called *teaching*. It is not about tricks; it is about a worldview. It should be about what they need to know to live in the world of humans and what they need to learn in order to more fully enjoy life. The behaviors taught today are a mash-up of those important for safety and for the sanity of the human, totally unimportant for any reason, possibly offensive, and actually fun for dog and person. What I want to teach Quid, most of all, is how to be a dog in this family in this place in this time—while still letting her be her unruly self. Maybe that last part is something I have to learn.

Some things the puppy has eaten/chewed that are not for eating/chewing: an observational study

ROCKS

DEER POOP

STICK BITS

BIT OF FLUFF FROM MY POCKET

PANTS

CAT'S EARS

FINGERNAILS

MY FINGER

HUMAN HAIR

HER OWN PAW

WOODCHUCK (No woodchucks were harmed.)

WALL

WINDOWSILLS

WINDOW HANDLE

INSECT WALKING ACROSS THE FLOOR

MOTHS

PENCIL TIPS

PENCIL ERASERS

BLACK ROLLERBALL PENS

DRIED LEAVES (after shredding them into a thousand slivery pieces first)

DIRT

SOFA ARMS

PILLOW

RUG

DOG CRATE

DOG BED

HER OWN LEASH

ICICLES

CARROT ENDS, CELERY ENDS, ASPARAGUS ENDS, KALE STALKS, STRAWBERRY TOPS

STRING

FLASHLIGHT

COMPASS

DRYER BALLS

VACUUM HOSE

COVER OF PAPERBACK BOOK

FIRST THIRTY-ONE PAGES OF BOOK

BOOKMARK IN BOOK

BOTTOM EDGE OF BOOK

BOOK

APRIL ✻ WEEK 12
Ghosts

'm typing w left hand as rt hand is unfer pup cannot be both-terred to ck ctyps.

I am extracted from captivity by the puppy when someone opens a door; she beelines to see who. Three months old, Quid has slid neatly into the family. And as she has relaxed into this space, her particular spirit is bubbling up.

On a walk today she neatly leaps from the paved path onto the horizontal rail of the fence lining the path. It is like a bird aloft: without preamble, she just takes flight. Back on the ground she finds a stick as long as she is and carries it proudly, head held high. With the stick in her mouth, she whines continually, working through some inner conflict unclear to us.

These glimpses of an inexplicable character are charming: we are seeing more of who she is. And at the same time, as with all young things, who she is is changing. Physically, she is bigger: still only twelve pounds, but her paws have begun looking pleasingly large compared to her body. Her ears continue skyward, and each day brings the game of Up or Down? as we chart their develop-ment into perked or folded. Today one is up and one is down. She is overly cute—like a stuffed toy so realistic that it veers into the unsettling. Or maybe I am just wary of handing my heart to this young thing. I am waiting for the falling-in-love part to kick in.

After we adopted her, Amy began a Facebook group so that the siblings' families could keep up with one another. I am not on Facebook—but Quid is. We spend evenings scrolling through the photos of her siblings, marveling at their increasingly visible differences and their notable similarities. The biggest males are a full 50 percent larger than Quid. And we can see a division growing between the scruffy dogs and the smooth-coated, between the up ears and down ears. Some live in multidog families; others are singletons. People compare notes on the minutiae of new dogness: What are they feeding them? Where did you get that harness? What are people doing about car sickness? I find it comforting to see all the puppies, even as they grow out of the familiar dumplings they were to me—and to glimpse inside the homes of their people. As millions of people who adopted a dog while quarantined during the 2020 pandemic are surely feeling, there is a surprising loneliness to raising a puppy in isolation. Typically, life with a puppy is two-pronged: private and public. The struggles and pleasures of raising a wild animal—er, young dog—are mostly private.

Outside the house, though, being appended to a puppy is, in normal times, surprisingly transformative. Puppies, like babies, are attractants: strangers pause at seeing them, veer to your side, coo and squeal. They want to touch, talk to, and know everything about the puppy. They comment on their beauty; they smile at the two of you. They provide affirmation of what a great choice you have made. Your puppy's cuteness is an endorsement of your good judgment. In a pandemic this public dynamic is lost. No one approaches anyone within touching distance. Sequestered in a house a half mile from our nearest neighbors, we could go days without seeing anyone at all.

At home, Quid is being put through a rigmarole of exposures while still in her socialization period. Each day, of course, she is exposed to new things not of our design: the thunderstorm transforming the air, the chipmunk racing by her feet, a visiting raccoon. She has been serenaded by thunder in the distance, crashes in the kitchen, high winds, high wind chimes, and heavy rain. She has sauntered by tractors, faced down vacuums, heard a couple of sirens and an electric drill. She has taken it all in stride. So we add our own odd sensations for her to experience: setting her on the sisal cat scratcher or a sheet of aluminum foil, to feel that underfoot. We present a large box on its side; the dog bed, inverted; a yoga ball. When she touches any of them, we reward her, and soon she is touching the foil and box and bed and ball purposefully, looking at us for her medal. When we leave this household obstacle course in place, lo and behold, she finds herself walking over and into and through it all, making all sorts of ruckus. We reward her for that, too.

Outside, Ammon concocts a seesaw by nailing a plank to a stump on its side. We lure her close. Before I can encourage her onto it, she walks right up the down side unflinchingly. Flinches are for surprises; to the puppy, this is just the way the world is. Her easygoing nature allows her to take it in stride. She is less sure about the hammock, but with a treat she is soon the sphinx in netted canvas, being rocked by her minions. We check off items from trainer Sophia Yin's list of ways one should gently handle a pup to acclimate her: we touch her feet and ears, pinch and poke her skin, tap her nose, turn her on her back, pull her to our laps; we turn her momentarily upside down. We bring her out to visit any delivery people delivering. And we make ourselves into new people, pulling out hats, sunglasses, and a fake mustache to try to appear like strange strangers. We ride by on our bikes, don helmets and hoodies, carry umbrellas unnecessarily.

She steps into every new situation with the same confidence as her first step in the morning: complete. It is only when we bring out the ghosts that we get a hint of a new Quiddity.

The idea of exposing her to ghosts comes from a Swedish working-dog community. They regularly gather to test their dogs' reactions to novel stimuli, like gunshots, rapidly moving objects, and unknown people. Somewhere along the way, it must have been decided to expose them to ghostlike figures, as imagined by a low-budget Halloween costumer: people dressed in sheets covering their bodies and plastic buckets with holes for eyes over their heads, emerging slowly from hiding places.

Ogden gets to play the ghost. He dresses in a drapey hooded caftan, and we prepare by watching a video of professional dog-ghosting behavior. First the "ghost" walks slowly toward a dog, stops about twelve feet from them, then turns around. Throughout this performance, the dog's reaction is gauged. Part two is the big reveal: the dog's handler marches right up to the ghost, chats with him like they are old friends, and helps the ghost remove his costume. The dog's reaction to this turn of events is gauged again.

The Swedish Working Dog Association has ideas about what behavior they hope their dogs will show in response to the ghosts. I am less sure. I try to imagine what I would want Quid to do should a ghost emerge from our forest: Do I want her to simply accept the appearance of this apparition and calmly walk away? Should she instead chase and tackle this obviously bonkers (or, to keep an open mind, deceased) person? Should she look at me dubiously?

She doesn't do any of those things. Before we leave the house, Ogden walks into the forest, hides behind a tree, and waits for me to get into position with Quid. At my signal, he creeps out slowly, arms partially raised in front of him, half zombie—a spontaneous flourish. It takes Quid a moment to notice him. Her body tenses; she peers toward the forest, her ears tuned to the slightest rustle. When he creeps his next ghost-zombie creep, she is sure of what to do: bark like mad.

Per the playbook I approach the ghost directly, and we begin talking. Quid barks nonstop, a completely new development for her. Then I help Ogden disrobe so that it is clear to everyone, Quid included, who this ghost is. He is there to be seen, heard, and smelled. Quid is unconvinced, despite having spent dozens of hours in full-body contact with Ogden. We walk back to the house; she barks the whole way. Inside, once she has run out of barks, she spends the rest of the day looking at him out of the side of her eyes.

Puppy side-eye

Though our efforts at teaching Quid anything are scattered at best, she is spontaneously learning much that is useful in organizing our life together. She has learned to go to doors and sit or scratch to tell us she needs to be on the other side of the door. She is responsive to "Come!" even with some distractions. And, thrillingly, she has picked up "Wait": around here, it means being the polite one pausing at the open door to let someone else go through first. Many *people* I know have not picked up "Wait." She will sit down to be let into the house—which I consider an incredible feat of self-control. How one connects *Put your rump down* with *because then you will get to move* is beyond me. Conversely, "Stop barking"—another negative—is trickier to teach; we are positive reinforcing the heck out of *being quiet*, but I sense that something else is being learned, like *That person often has snacks in her pocket.* Some people teach "Quiet," or even teach "Speak," trying to route the bark to be on cue. For now, we are distracting her, trying to get her to do a behavior that is impossible to do while barking, like holding a toy or eating a treat.

Quid's training of us, on the other hand, is going fantastically well. I have learned to fill my pockets with peanut butter treats. I can be coaxed into rubbing her face merely by her looking at me pleadingly, ears laid back against her head. She has taught me to speak in an exceedingly high tone if I actually want her to come. She has trained Ogden to play with her by nosing him and nibbling his toes, and she has trained Ammon to collect good-looking sticks (diameter greater than an inch; length between one foot and three) for her.

The dogs are the best teachers of all. One evening I am walking back to the house and see the three of them—two dogs, one puppy—lined up at different windows of the porch, all sniffing outward with anticipation. It makes me wonder who this puppy would be if there had not been Finn and Upton in her life. They are her guides to doghood in our house: how the house runs, what the pace of the day is, where we wander—and what is allowed, expected, gotten away with, and appreciated. Each of the dogs deals with her differently, per their different natures; both of them are models of how to be.

⊱⊰

This month could be described as a protracted exercise in impulse control and learning to stop when your body says go. Just when she discovers squirrels, our puppy is also told *not* to chase that squirrel; as soon as she learns she can reach my mouth by jumping, she is told *not* to jump. Outside is full of important things to pursue, but *no*, we say *don't dart out the door*. And now that Quid lives in a land of bagels, for some reason she is not allowed to grab that bagel I am holding so tantalizingly close to her.

While we are contorting ourselves to try to get the puppy on board with living with us, without even trying the dogs keep showing her what to do. Dogs are drawn to where other dogs are, or to what they are doing. It is not quite the same as teaching, but it affords the chance for learning: the presence of one dog lets the second one notice that there is something or somewhere worth interacting with—like a smell in the grass or a treat on a table. One study on this phenomenon set up a room so that subject dogs could peek in on other dogs while they searched for food in various boxes. When all the dogs were reunited, the observing dogs made "snout contact" with the dogs they had watched; if the dog had found food, the observers raced to the location they had seen them searching.

The opportunities for this kind of social learning in a multidog household are constant. Not everything learned is what we would hope, though. A nonbarker can learn to bark by exposure to barkers; a cat's litter box can be discovered by following an experienced litter box visitor to the source. If one dog is allowed to get away with being on the bed, good luck keeping a second dog off it. There is a kind of learning from puppy to person, too, we have found. Thus we learn to follow the puppy when she quietly disappears from sight (usually followed by trouble) and to never open the door without first looking out for the birds or chipmunks that she is in search of.

Quid has also made us aware of how we talk to her—the words that get through to her and those that are not heard. *Come* is an arbitrary assignment of sounds to mean something like *move your body over here.* There is nothing about it that compels someone to move; nothing that models any part of movement. But when we use the word, we assume that a dog will get it. It takes great effort not to use full sentences with the puppy: *Not now—we'll go out later, after dinner.* Even knowing that we are just talking to ourselves, we still use those sentences. But I think that deep down we are a little surprised or put off when they do not understand.

Research has shown that dogs have a dedicated voice area in their brain that responds specifically to sounds from other dogs, just as we have for sounds from other humans. And dogs appear to be more responsive to sounds from nondog sources (like people) than we are to nonpeople sources. Adult dogs get so good at recognizing their names that they can hear their name when spoken by a stranger across a room full of noisy talking. Bring your dog to your next birthday party and try it.

Of course I am talking nonstop to Quid. "Hi, little one. Scooch! Okay! Let's go pee!" When she pulls ahead, straining to free her body from the harness and beeline for the squirrel, my way of communicating to her my displeasure is to say "You're not helping." It is not that I am completely oblivious to her noncomprehension; I feel certain that we simply narrate our lives out loud with our dogs.

Though this habit means we miss the chance to actually talk to her in a way she will understand—through our behavior.

We have gotten one thing right, at least. Almost automatically, when we talk to dogs, we use higher-pitched tones than when we are talking to humans. Puppy-directed speech is highest of all. And it turns out that puppies, more than adult dogs, are really responsive to this kind of speech: they react more reliably and faster, and approach the speaker more often, than if the same request is given in normal human-directed tones. We also slow down the speed of our speech when talking to dogs; we articulate our vowels more—similar to when people talk to their babies. Ogden has gone one step further and begun calling Quid with the high *hoo-hoo hoo-hoooo* of the local barred owls. She is the only one he talks to in owl language. It works.

As the puppy grows ever more into herself, I find myself musing a lot about her appearance. Just as we carefully noted the puppies' weight in the first weeks of their lives, each new sprout of hair, tail feather, or coy look of Quid's is noted and recorded. It is as though we are reassuring ourselves that she is still cute. An Australian study of dogs and their people found that people who have a strong relationship with their dogs also see them as cuter. In other words, just as we unfairly do with people, we rate dogs by their cover.

Fifty things you should notice about your puppy

1. how she looks at you
2. how you look at her
3. the precise day she learns to associate the crinkle of a plastic bag with food
4. the evolution of her nose from pink to black
5. the evolution of her eyes from blue to whatever-they-become
6. the ratio of black whiskers to white whiskers
7. when her incisors come in
8. which side she likes to lie on (Quid: left-leaning)
9. where she likes to rest in a room, vis-à-vis you and any other humans and dogs; whether it is in the sun or on the hard floor or by the door
10. the progression of toe pads from pink to dark (today: one pink on front right foot, two on back right foot)
11. what punctuation mark the tail most resembles
12. where she likes to be tickled
13. where she doesn't like to be tickled
14. when she realizes that her tail is following her
15. when she barks; what you do when she barks; whether she continues to bark nonetheless
16. which paw she uses first to descend the stairs; which paw she uses to ask you for something; which paw she uses to pin down a squeaky toy to begin its evisceration
17. when she coordinates the rear legs and front legs

18. nonbarking, nongrowling sounds she makes (as of this week: *arooo*, snuffling in play, whimper-sigh when settling down to rest, whimper-cry when holding on to a precious ball or stick)

19. the warmth of her belly

20. how the room sounds when she is in it with you

21. the sound of her running up the stairs to attack you on the bed in the morning

22. the precise number and names of all the colors of her fur

23. eyebrows: their existence

24. her noseprint: the unique shape of the front of her nose

25. how her head smells

26. how the pads of her feet smell

27. the tiniest eyelashes

28. the sweetness of sleep

29. how she corners (skidding, slowly, rump glancing the ground)

30. whom she looks to when she needs something

31. how she tells you she needs something

32. how she can scooch forward with limbs extended out front and behind

33. what makes her happy

34. what scares her

35. how high she can jump; how much higher that is than she is

36. the ways of her ears

37. when she overtakes you in land-running speed

38. her opinion about her own shadow: friend or foe?

39. the staccato exhales as she relaxes into sleep

40. how her ears can move independently

41. when she realizes birds can fly, and squirrels can go up trees

42. the part of the house she doesn't yet know exists

43. when she notices the puppy in the mirror

44. different ways to sit: sphinx, George Booth dog, rump barely on floor

45. how she looks without a collar

46. how she looks when she's wet

47. which thing you don't want her to eat that she's most interested in eating

48. sleep-suckling

49. sleep-barking

50. how happy she is you're back

APRIL ❀ WEEK 13
Puppy's Point of View

"Shelter in place!" Ogden yells as we dive for his bed and pull the blanket over our heads. Quick on our heels we hear the distinctive rapid *tick-tick-tick-tick* of small-dog toenails on wood floors. And then she is upon us, hurtling onto the bed and snuffling us out under the covers. Both dogs come down and play with her, everyone feeling good and up for some open-mouthed wrestling. Watching them play puts a huge smile on my face.

We are all affected by the pleasure of late spring: of being able to be outside without coats and hats, of a breeze on bare arms and legs. Quid has gained a few inches in height, and her body is filling out into more sausage than dumpling. But she is impressively little among the dogs. Her scruffy fur is emerging weed-like, everywhere and often. It is coming out of her eyebrows; it is in the crook of her ears; it is popping out from between the tiny pink pads of her feet.

This is the week we put the GoPro camera on her. Having spent my career trying to understand the dog's point of view, it is only a matter of time before the dogs in my household get the action-camera treatment. While it does not pass for mind reading, a good first step in understanding someone's worldview is to simply get to their height and go at their pace.

Quid barely flinches as we put the tiny camera on the back of her harness. It sits atop her shoulder blades, giving us a view of the white blaze on the back of her neck and her giant ink-black ears, mightily working to stay erect.

As soon as the camera is on, Ammon runs out into the forest, prompting Quid to charge after him. Ogden and I watch on my phone, connected to the camera, as the back of Ammon's legs and shoes come into sight and disappear as she catches and passes him quickly. The camera gives us a dizzying view of bouncing ears as the world wobbles by at high speeds, punctuated by pauses when she turns her gaze to the ground, to her feet, to the sky, as though attempting to collect every detail of her surroundings. There are long periods amid tall grasses. We call her back to us. As she gears up for another run, we can nearly feel her full head shake: ten complete cycles in a second and a half, from left ear to the sky to right ear to the sky.

We can see how her attention flits, drawn by a chipmunk chirp, a stirring in the fallen leaves, or something imperceptible to us. More startling, perhaps, is to realize, via the camera, how often we are at the center of her gaze. Towering figures, we are gesturing and smiling and making mouth noises. Sometimes our arms extend suddenly and touch her head or curl a finger around her collar. When we start moving away, she is nearly compelled to follow. We have begun to be her sun.

This peek into her perspective makes it easier to imagine what she is experiencing as we walk with her. I put my nose in the direction of the breeze that hits us; I keep my eye on the stone wall where we saw chipmunks that one time; I take note of all the acorns on the ground that she might mouth. I am under no illusion that I know what it is like to be her, but I have started seeing into her world.

As we imagine into her point of view, I wonder if Quid has a sense of who she is and where she comes from. It is time to try to visit a sibling. I message Annie, who adopted Acorn—still named Acorn—and who lives less than an hour away. We are still knee-deep in the pandemic, but outdoors is starting to feel relatively safe. We agree to meet in a little park not far from where she lives.

Quid, Ogden, and I arrive just as Annie is approaching the park on foot with Acorn. He is about Quid's size, tan, with the same white paint on his tail, legs, and snout—and completely scruffy. He has a full beard, quite distinguished for a four-month-old puppy. His ears are folded upon themselves, giving him a charmingly rumpled look. We hop out of the car, and Quid barks a hello, causing Acorn to turn and head toward us.

Their noses meet, and their bodies tense with excitement. They have lived apart as long as they lived together. I am alert for any sign that they recognize each other. I see . . . nothing. Not, at least, before they run off into the field and begin playing together. They quickly start a game of chasing-fleeing-tackling-biting-somersaulting, alternating roles. Watching Acorn makes me see Quid better, in noting their differences. She is a practitioner of the bite-scruff-jump-on style of play; he is more of a self-take-down kind of guy, pushing his head into the ground and flinging his body down after it. Her run is accomplished with serious intent, whereas he teeter-totters, enjoying the moment. But these are little differences. I finally see their recognition of each other: it is in the ease with which they began to play at all. With barely an introduction, they just picked up where they had left off two months ago, when one morning brought a series of cars and a disappearance of siblings.

🦴

While for humans the first three years are full of memorable events—learning how to walk, where mommy or daddy usually is, how to say *dog*—people typically cannot later remember back to that time. Our memory systems are still in development, and though we can later recall the how—to walk, to talk—the lived experience of that learning is lost. One wonders whether it is the same for puppies. When Quiddity sees her brother, they likely do not share reminiscences about their early weeks on the towel with mom. That said, their behavior toward each other is different from that toward an entirely unknown dog: the littermates seem to recognize each other on some level, in a way perhaps not consciously available to them.

Even without consciously knowing if someone is a family member or not, most animals have a way to avoid inbreeding with a relative. For dogs, that is likely by smell. When dogs were presented with the odor of their siblings (collected from the towel on which they lay at night), without their siblings actually being present, one study found that pups who now lived with other, unrelated dogs could recognize their relatives.

Eventually this skill translates to recognition of their people, too. Dogs who were separated from their person for up to three years

THE YEAR OF THE PUPPY

preferred to spend time with a tug toy or towel with their person's scent—the scent left by their hand—than with one a stranger of the same sex had held.

By four months puppies are thinking of people as *their* people. They show classic attachment behaviors—distress at separation, delight at reunion. Dogs have evolved to, perhaps, show more attachment to the people who adopt them than to the mother who birthed them. They attach to us—and quickly: adult dogs in a shelter who receive three ten-minute visits from a person start showing signs of attachment behavior.

Without our noticing it, Quid has slipped into the next stage of her young life. While we tend to call any dog under the age of one year a puppy, strictly speaking they have matured out of puppyness at about twelve weeks. Now she is a few weeks into the juvenile period, which starts where the socialization period left off and lasts until puberty, several months away. It is still a wildly formative time in their lives: their brains are continuing to change in response to their experiences. Weirdly, though, dogs of this age have not been widely studied. Anecdotally we know that events during the juvenile period can affect their behavior into adulthood—in other species, it is clear that certain abilities are set during this time and become inflexible—but scientifically, they are basically off the map.

What research there is has focused on the continued impor- tance of socialization, even outside the socialization period. In one study a group of guide dogs in training were socialized to humans until they left the litter at twelve weeks old. Then, for the next several weeks, half of them went to kennels, where they saw very few people; the other half were placed in homes. When tested later on whether they had the skills to graduate to be guide dogs, the kenneled dogs more often failed—and more failed with each extra week in the kennel. Many failed because they were frightened of people and new things, thus not suited to the life of a guide dog, who must constantly be among new people.

While most dogs do not need to pass guide dog tests to be terrific companions, this finding attests that even good training can be undone by time in an impoverished environment—say, being left alone in a kennel or in an understaffed shelter without enrichment programs.

"Puppy classes"—where many pups are given a chance to socialize—are often recommended during this time, though it is not clear that these, rather than other factors in the dogs' lives, have any particular positive effect on the dogs' future behavior. Nor is there any evidence that they are harmful. But given how different these classes are from place to place, it is clear that they ought not to be used as a substitute for regular exposures to new things, animals, and people.

At the Working Dog Center, this period of time is a chance to try some of those novel exposures with the pups, who are now each fostered in a separate home and come to the Penn campus for testing. There, Dana graduates them to a more rigorous practice, the next step on the way to being trained to find odors. The pups are taller and lankier than when I saw them last. Vara (previously Yellow) is the first dog out of the gate and arrives with a gaily wagging tail. She conquers the flirt pole—now flirted over a slick surface—like a professional fisherman. A rattle can, now a milk jug with coins in it, is tossed across the room. As Vara bounds after it, Dana drops a two-by-four to the ground, making me jump in my seat. Dana laughs: that is the idea—to see if that startling sound dissuades Vara from her pursuit of the exciting milk jug. It does not: she does not even wince. She merrily carries the jug by the handle, head held high. She throws it down, drops herself after it, and begins gnawing, her tail explosively happy. Finally Dana jingles a set of keys and drops them in a wheeled metal cart. Vara jumps into the cart without a pause, like a professional cart-jumper-upper. "You got it! My goodness! Good giiirrrllll!" Dana coos. Vara is ready for the next set of tests that she and all the pups will take outside over the next months, exposing her to a greater variety of odd sounds, places, and people—mimicking what working dogs might encounter in their lives.

MAY ❀ WEEK 14
In and Up

The grasses in the meadow have grown faster than Quid has; they now tower over her. From her vantage, she is facing a verdant wall of green and refuses to enter it—or perhaps does not see that there is any way in. Upton forges through, and I follow him.

She not only doesn't get in, she doesn't get up. Despite the heights Quid can jump, in the house we can still disappear from her world entirely—and give the dogs a reprieve from puppy attention—by going upstairs. Each of the eleven steps to the second floor is eight inches high but may as well be a mountain. She looks after us for a moment but then walks away. We are just on the moon. Will be back later.

Quid finally takes the plunge into the grasses, mustering the biggest leap she can: Full Puppy Intensity is necessary to get in there. Soon she is bounding through the fields, neatly beheading dandelions with her mouth as she goes. Each time she dips under the green horizon, her ears are the last part of her to disappear.

Those ears. We are still monitoring her ears every day. Daughter of an Australian cattle dog mix, she may have giant erect ears in her DNA; we can't know yet, though, since each day they tell a different tale. Today both ears are erect and gently folded over at the tips—though one pops up when the last of the food is being scraped off the dinner plate. We gather a surprising expertise in the flag language of ears. There are the half-mast ears, which rise up—only to fold back on themselves, asymmetrical—one up and one down; full mast, completely pricked; the rose ear, half-mast and pinned back; button ears, totally flopped. We can't make sense of their development. One day they salute; the next they bow under their own weighty effort. We scrutinize the photos of her siblings for their ear fates. Each of the pups of the litter has differently directed ears, compass signs to varying life paths.

As invested as we all are in the minutiae of her life, my friend Daniel laughs at me gently when I describe how it's going with the puppy and start off by saying I don't love her yet. I do like her, I say. I just do not know her well enough yet. My guardedness doesn't just have to do with her; it's about how it changes the nature of our whole family.

With Quid, we did not just adopt a puppy, we completely disrupted everyone's lives in the house, including those of the other animals. My relationship with Finn, with Upton, the dogs' relationship with each other—everyone's relationship with everyone else—is changed by this addition. And every moment of all our days is changed.

Getting a puppy also changes us. Ogden has a brand-new smile: an ingenuous, big-toothed smile. I am vigilant: underslept, worried about the future ramifications of a growl here, an urge to run there. Ammon, already unflappable, now epitomizes the phrase "taking things in stride."

For the animals, Quid's arrival has consolidated some of their most endearing traits and birthed some new ones. Finn wears the face he had as a puppy, with a steady, earnest excitement that surprises me. For the first time ever, he jumps out of bed in the morning and heads down the treacherously steep stairs before me—in order to see (and growl at) Quid. Upton oversees great open-mouthed play bouts, in which he is the friendly teacher looming over his young student. Edsel's early feline overtures were met with such gusto that she now sits on the highest perches in the house, guardedly watching the puppy. Both she and Upton have ways of looking away disdainfully from an overexcited puppy that are quite effective.

"You know," Ogden says one morning, "having a puppy is awesome, but it really makes you appreciate your time with the other animals." The dogs' pace is familiar, pleasant—under control. Quid runs headlong into the day, hurtling her body into the new space. By providing a constant contrast, living with the puppy allows us to see the other animals better. This might be the thing I do already love about Quid: her arrival changed the scene before us. Everyone's individuality is heightened.

Living with a new dog is a reminder of how much of what we think about dogs is speculation, inklings, glimpses, and suggestion—not based on the plain reality of you and a dog alone together in a room, looking at each other.

To counter our hesitation we have been playing a game developed by the trainer Kathy Sdao. As visible as the puppy's difficult behaviors are, every moment between them is filled with pretty desirable behaviors. Sdao's idea is to bother to look for these behaviors and reward them in the classic positive-reinforcement way (with a happy *Yes!* and a tasty treat). Do it fifty times in a day, and you are forced to see all the good behaviors she is already doing—and encourage them. "Start with any behavior that is simply not annoying," Sdao says helpfully. I look at Quid at my feet, asleep. I kind of love that. *Yes!* I wake her up and offer a little treat. She looks puzzled, but I feel better already. She notices the goldfinches outside fluttering around a bird feeder and does not bark or run at them or do anything but look and sniff. *Yes!* She wags and cocks her head. *Yes!*

For me the end result of this kind of activity is to suddenly notice all her non-annoyingness. I am reminded of the hopefulness of getting a puppy during the pandemic: The assumption that we will get to grow together as a family. That there are things to look forward to, plan for, hope for. What a lot of hopes to put on a little puppy.

It is about this time that I realize that, because of the pandemic, our dogs are nearly the only dogs she has interacted with for more than a few minutes since we adopted her. Even knowing the importance of exposing her to new dogs, we have mostly not. Our outings to a local park, famous for dog walking, have been our concession—but even there, most people do not want to get close enough to meet a puppy on a leash. Quid has met a sweet pit bull, a couple of other young puppies, a pair of lovely drooly bloodhounds. Maybe a half dozen more. Most only for a few minutes. Nothing near what a life in that hopeful future will bring, dog-wise.

So we go to meet Caine, a very large, sweet, energetic eight-year-old boxer. His greeting leap, begun at a modest gallop, will knock me down. Caine's people, our friends, invite us to walk with them in the meadows outside their home.

On arrival at her first-ever new-dog playdate, we learn that Quid has hackles: fully down her back to her tail. They appear promptly after Caine approaches us with his usual enthusiasm. Quid hides under me. She growls a little, barks, and ignores the treats offered to her. By contrast, Caine seems delighted, romping in circles around us, politely not crowding her, just keeping an interested eye in our direction. Quid stands around growling, her eyes fixed on Caine.

Ten minutes into this I finally suggest we begin walking along their meadow. I drop Quid's leash so she can move at her own pace. And at that moment the entire dynamic is changed. At once she is chasing and being chased by Caine, jumping on him and letting him bound over her. They race ahead of us, disappear over the hill, and return running in parallel. Their relationship has gone from "lightly hostile" to "best friends" in sixty seconds. So goes the next half hour.

That is how I am reminded that it is easier to meet a dog while moving. Our normal human social encounter has us stopping and facing one another. For dogs, this may simply be too much. Quid's approach is more as if we met someone new and just started running madly along with them, occasionally tagging them and racing away screaming. A game that, I think to myself, she wouldn't be unhappy if we played with her ourselves.

ᛉ

With our eyes on her ears, we have missed being witness to the biggest growth happening in front of us: the transition of her body out of puppy shape and closer to adult shape. She will continue to gain muscles for the next few years, but by fourteen weeks or so, her body shape is halfway to full dogness.

Dogs' bodies mature in what is called a craniocaudal direction, meaning head to rump. The puppy head starts out quite large—part of what makes them look cute, with their heads out of proportion to their bodies. After early puppyhood, most dogs' heads don't grow much, while the rest of their body catches up. Maturing dogs go from plump to longer and slimmer.

Their legs develop at different rates, too. Just as the head beats the rump, the front legs mature faster than the back legs. This gives puppies their appealing, bounding gait—one that is also likely tiring, so they may need to suddenly rest in the middle of a walk. And the top segment of the leg, the kind of "upper arm," grows faster than the lower segment. The most stable adult dog body has an even length of each of the three segments, once the forearm grows out.

As she grows, the puppy has to adjust to a world that feels as if it is changing size, too. The cat bed she fit in during her first week with us, she no longer fits in. But she is still trying to squeeze into it. Similarly for laps and safe spots under the couch. Despite their rapid growth, though, dogs adapt spectacularly well to their changeable environment. In our lab's own research, we have found that dogs trying to get through a doorway when we repeatedly decrease its height have a good sense of what they can fit through, given the size of their bodies. They might try to fit through too small a space but rarely attempt it more than once or twice before trying another method. Most dogs use a similar series of adjustments to squeeze through an increasingly small doorway: first ducking their heads, then bending their elbows, and finally, if necessary, corkscrewing their bodies to the side.

So maybe their insistence on sitting on your lap when they are grown, and no longer lap-size, is due not so much to a lack of awareness of their own size. They know how large they are. It simply has to do with their love of your lap.

As she grows in stature and becomes more proportional, we start seeing how that affects the height Quid can jump—and also the full spread of gaits that are seen in most adult dogs. From her very first steps with us, she was doing the classic dog walk—the slow gait in which each side's rear limb chases the forelimb: rear right, front right, rear left, front left. Three feet are always on the ground. With puppies, though, movement escalates into a run pretty quickly; the run is called a gallop if they achieve full flight for a moment, all legs off the ground. As a small dog, walking on leash alongside one of us, Quid trots: the opposite legs move together—front right with rear left. On each side, the step of the rear leg more or less hits the same spot as the front leg does.

We are used to this now—to our puppy's gallopy, leaping ways. As she matures, we are also getting more of a hint of what effect a global pandemic might have on her and dogs like her. Through our only consistent connection with others—online—we began hearing about a new phenomenon: *pandemic pets*, the media began to call them, as though they themselves were a rampant virus. Our society was suddenly connected by the shared experiences of those now dealing for the first time with a companion animal. In fact, though, nearly 330,000 fewer animals were adopted in 2020 than in the previous year, a 17 percent drop. But rates of dog purchases may have increased. (Sales numbers are not tracked in the same way.) A very real phenomenon for all these pets, though, is the unusual glimpse that they are getting of human society. Early development is a time when a puppy can learn how the human world works—only it is not really working now. What is visible to dogs is the experience of the pandemic that we wear: we are wearing masks, and we are wearing our anxiety.

It is not long into the widespread acceptance of mask-wearing when I begin to be asked if dogs can recognize us while we are masked. While I have been surprised to not recognize a few familiar people with their masks on, I am more surprised at how many I can recognize. In a recent study from our lab, we presented dogs with the smell of their persons—absent the presence of the person—to see if they could distinguish it from other people's smells. To gather the "person smell," we asked one person in a two-person dog household to wear a new cotton T-shirt for two nights without washing it, washing themself, or using any fragrances—including soap and lotion. Our shirts capture the very normal odor that humans effuse all the time, which is detectable to our nose but that we do not usually consciously take in. Dutifully following our instructions, the T-shirt wearers then stuffed the shirt in a large Ziploc bag, sealed it, and gave it to us. When the second person in the household came to our lab with their dog, we presented the dogs with the stinky T-shirts—as well as with a T-shirt from a stranger who had performed the same routine. By timing how long they sniffed each one, we found that the dogs had no trouble distinguishing their person's odor from a stranger's.

If a dog knows who you are without your even being present, your having a mask on is not terribly confusing to them. That said, to identify us by smell, they must be relatively close to us—or we have to be extra stinky and have a breeze at our backs. Dogs are much better readers of our bodies than we are of theirs; we tend to focus too much on people's heads. Dogs do look at our faces, too. A recent spate of studies on how dogs perceive human emotions found that they are good at distinguishing happy faces from blank expressions and happy from angry faces (preferring the former, of course), can match a photo of an angry or happy face with a vocalization in the same emotional valence, and can use the happy or disgusted face of a person opening a box to choose wisely which box to approach themselves. And they can identify these expressions even when presented with a photo of only the top half of the face—in other words, with the part that they can still see when we are masked. They are just as good with top-half faces as with full faces.

The only downside of our wearing masks that I can see for dogs is that we are providing less lovely food-breath odor for them to sniff.

For now, being young during a pandemic is Quid's reality and the condition at hand. Perhaps the best we can do is see her as she is now. I gently pull my foot out from under a sleeping puppy's head and turn off the computer to go to bed.

Height Puppy Can Jump: An Alarming Growth Curve

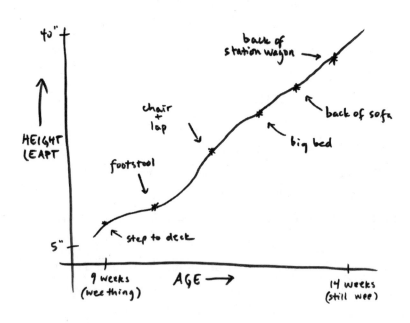

JUNE ❀ WEEK 20
The Troubles

She is running in a distant field, ears levitating with each step. She is already a more mature dog, longer of limb and firmer of body. Five months old, she has lived longer with us than she did with her litter. Ogden has become tall and gangly, too, right before my eyes. While Quid's white whiskers are turning black—reverse aging—Finn's black muzzle is streaked with white hairs, the backs of his legs now woven with gray.

Time has folded into itself: the isolation induced by the pandemic leaves us without clear markers for the days, and we have lost our sense of the date. Every now and then we realize that another month has passed. So we wake up each morning surprised to see a slightly different puppy.

Our days are punctuated only by how long it has been since the puppy was out, when she last ate, the last time we threw a ball for her or hid some treats for a treasure hunt. Her daily needs and weekly development give us our bearings. Still, the ten weeks of early puppyhood, when so much was happening, contrast with the ten weeks she has been with us, when every day is an eerie variation of the previous.

The variations are concerning. Quid's behavior is mercurial—it is as if she could become a new puppy each morning. One day she is brave and confident, charging through a fence to greet a dog on the other side; another she is shy and unsure, hiding between my legs when a woman comes to say hello. She alerts, hackles up, at a man in the far distance walking along but then also wags and licks at the face of another who holds out a finger for her to sniff. It is as though her sense of categories is in flux: Is this friend or foe? Should I bark or should I hide?

Recently, she has elected to bark. At three months she began barking at unknown dogs and people—and at anything notable at all. She barks when she plays, when she runs, when she hears a car pass. When a bird lands on the bird feeder, when a plane flies overhead.

Too, she has become what I would describe as *fixated* on little furry things. Her fondness for chasing squirrels has extended to chipmunks. And mice. And voles and woodchucks and rats and any other scurrying thing. She cries piteously when I leash her, ignores me as I try to entice her with a treat or a run. Once she has spotted someone, she must chase.

Her enthusiasm in the house has grown in scale. She has begun play-biting—a lot. And hard. At times she looks at Ogden and growls. If we pay her no heed, she goes and finds the cat and incites her.

It's troubling.

It is not undoglike, of course. What is troubling is that the literature suggests that single events in this period can change how puppies respond to whole classes of stimuli. My first-love dog, Pumpernickel, was accidentally outside in a thunderstorm one day; until she blissfully lost some of her hearing in her old age, she was terrified of incoming storms. The puppy who receives an overly sharp nip from an annoyed adult dog may be reluctant to approach another dog for years.

With Quid, I have no concern about her being afraid. Her world has thus far been friendly and safe. The trouble is not whether she will do okay. It is whether she is ready for this world—and the world for her, for that matter. I am concerned for the small dog who reminds her of a squirrel—to say nothing of the squirrel—the child innocently going by on a bike, the overfriendly neighbor who reaches to pet *such a cute little head*. Quid is set on high, and the rest of us are running at medium low.

I realize we need to re-up her socialization, to further expand her universe. We start with a small upstate town, Hudson, New York, whose main street is usually lined with strolling pedestrians popping in and out of its coffee shops and antique furniture stores. In the warm early evening of a summer's day, we drive there. We have not visited for many months. While the pandemic has loosened its grip on us somewhat, we see on approach that the sidewalks are fairly empty. With our windows down I hear little but our own car. All the better to take things slow with Quid—for whom this sleepy version of a city will be the first version of any sort.

While we find the town to be decidedly quiet, Quid is agog. I listen more carefully, and there are lots of sounds she has never experienced: a mailbox clanking as it swallows a letter, a walk sign ticking down the seconds, an unmuffled car cruising by. The train along the river, a mile away, hoots its arrival. A thick smell of heat radiating off the asphalt colors the air. Every minute or so someone appears ahead on the sidewalk, which begins a little routine. I see the person; I see Quid see the person. She prepares to go on high alert. That is when I ply her with a stream of tiny treats, and we continue on, my hand near her mouth, until the person is blissfully past. Ten minutes of this and she is exhausted—as am I. It is effortful to notice everything. She naps all the way home.

The next day we try Great Barrington, a town of similar size— and similarly ghost-towny compared to its usual activity. But then we hit the gold mine: the hardware store. Its doors are propped open; inside are three clerks and two or three customers strolling the wide aisles. They light up at the sight of her. They approach. Quid freezes. I freeze. They make the sounds of people seeing a cute puppy. I ply cute puppy with treats, which she takes from the side of her mouth while staring down the approaching clerks. They are three young women, and they walk toward us in a very nonthreatening, indirect way. They murmur at her; Quid cocks her head. I could not have designed better new people to meet. Quid lets them close, they get some petting in, and she gets a metric ton of treats over the course of three minutes. She is now looking to us when she feels wary—and expecting a treat. We oblige.

This small victory emboldens me. It is time, I decide, to go to the Big City.

While we cannot expect New York City's usual crowds, the unending construction noise, the reliable runways of dogs being walked from apartment house to park and back, I am optimistic. We have to imagine it from Quid's point of view. To her, *everything* is new and incredibly surprising. She has never seen high-rise buildings. Elevators. Miles of sidewalks. Sidewalks with people, sidewalks with people and dogs and pigeons and trash cans. The sheer number of people on even a quiet street. The sounds—the backing-up truck, a door slamming, a metal gate being raised or lowered. And the smells!

Driving into the city, I look at Quid in the back seat, her body curled into a round dog bed, and wonder if it will be too much. I promise her sleeping form that we will leave if it is overwhelming. After parking I take a final look at Quid before I put a leash on her and introduce her to the city where we live. She looks ready.

And then she encounters all the things. There is person after person—some appearing suddenly from between cars or from surprising metal portals to the underground. Some have hats, canes, are in motorized wheelchairs, are very small people who run directly at her and try to pick her up. Faces mostly have masks, and some have hair flowing down their chins. Some smell quite profoundly strong, even to the person on the other end of the leash. There are things on the sidewalk: Paper bag? Check. Fast-food wrapper? Check. Plastic bag lofting gently in the breeze? Check. Pigeons are a new kind of giant bird that are nearly her size. There are very daring squirrels who stare her down and saunter off only one Quid-snout length from us. The ground itself is a kind of permanently tough grass—the sidewalk holds all its secrets in layers on top, not buried deep down. Then there is the asphalt, bearing giant noisy animals that roll and make a vaguely threatening rumble. Cars. Taxis. Buses. All are new and fascinating.

There are rocks to climb, trees to sniff, running people who she assumes want to be chased, right? She gets no encouragement from me. She tries anyway.

There are other dogs—so many dogs. We meet: Puddles, Milo. Stella. Poe. We meet giant dogs, fluffy dogs, doodles, more doodles. Dogs in baby strollers, twin dachshunds, three-legged dogs. We meet an inordinate number of wide-eyed puppies—and dog people with various degrees of wide-eyedness themselves.

Even over the course of a few days, my own perception is changed to notice the things she might be alarmed by. I, like her, take notice of each person in the distance—the very large or small kid on a scooter, scootering wildly, or with an especially big helmet. I fixate on things I have learned to ignore from living in the city for years: motorcycles, a screaming man raging down the street, a larger-than-expected rat. I know that at seven o'clock people will lean out their windows to clap, to ring cowbells, to shout their gratitude for first responders working in the pandemic; Quid does not and, on hearing the clamor, looks at me expectantly. And then I see that she is turning to me at other times, too, which is basically telling me that she is noticing something that she feels unsure about—so I find whatever is unnerving her and we bravely walk past it together.

Quid's smallness—combined with her big ears—turns a lot of heads. As people reach down a hand or want to pat her head, she ducks and weaves out of the way. At the same time, she is curious to approach and close-sniff each person. (Some of them veer out of the way, too.) And I learn that she has conquered the leash to the point where she is now ignoring it completely. The best moment this morning is before 9:00 a.m., when dogs are permitted off leash in the city parks. I drop her leash and she flies toward a handful of dogs at play on a park hill. For all her isolation, Quid shows no hesitation with these brand-new dogs and is soon caught up in a zoomy run with a smiling yellow Lab and a small black puppy. For a moment I relax. She is just a good pup.

On the way home, as the crowds clear the park, she sees a single person in the distance and barks a single shrill bark. Then looks at me expectantly for a treat.

🦴

To amateur ears, barks are just noise. But *noisy* does not mean meaningless. Barking is communication, and our reaction to this noise—to shush it or punish it—is more or less like slapping a child for talking unbidden.

What are dogs talking about? Barks convey a lot of emotional information—there are barks to induce play and barks barked when alone; there are barks to announce a stranger and barks used as a request. It is notable that barking is right smack in the frequency range of human speech—and may be an attempt to talk with us in a way we could understand. Wolves, dogs' nearest relatives, rarely bark. Dog barks are certainly pitched to get our attention.

The dog person's concern—*will they bark all the time?*—is a real one, given the societal view on barking. Yet that quiet puppy in the other room: watch out. One of Quid's early lesson plans for us had her being perfectly quiet. After ten minutes we realized that we could neither hear nor see the puppy. We found her in Ogden's room, methodically disemboweling a Sharpie. Often, quietness indicates mischief.

Many people's instinct when a dog barks loudly is to yell a stern *No!* or *Stop it!* But when we do this, we are responding with a kind of bark right back at the dog. It is funny, and a little sad, that we do this, since their barks are not angry yells but messages with content. Now, the *No!* might work for a moment (*What is she barking about?* their cocked heads seem to say), but this is not a long-term way of getting a dog not to bark. The dog's behavior indicates that they do not understand *no* as meaning *no barking, please*, but rather take it as general scolding. In the face of barking, those in the know keep quiet.

This is not to say that dogs do not have a sense of what *no* means; any dog who has been on the receiving end of a human's angry *No!* surely does. They understand the anger of it—if not exactly which thing they are doing we might be angry about.

While dogs will never become fluent language users, we weirdly downplay their own communications. Quid, at five months, will never say *mama* to me, but she has different whines and barks for needing to go outside, wanting attention, feeling disturbed at the cat's taking her bed, and requesting more tickling of ears; she knows the difference between *wait* and *stay*; she knows not just her name but the names of Finn and Upton. She lies *down* when I ask her to get *down off the bed*—not so much a misunderstanding, I would say, as a commentary on our often vague and confusing requests of dogs.

At the Working Dog Center, Vara, aka Yellow, has a different experience with barking: when she does come out with her shrill, insistent bark, the trainers shower her with praise. Amritha Mallikarjun sends me videos of each member of the *V* litter in their sixth month. Long and lanky, Vara is clambering over wooden pallets, lightly navigating a pile of cement rubble. She gallops by a school bus with its hood open and stop sign permanently out, then trots back and starts nosing around various large pipes. She halts at one and starts barking repetitively, her tail broadly wagging. Surprisingly, a person pops out from behind a barrier and shrieks her praise, while also holding out a rope to tug. This is the live-person search, in which the dogs are asked to find the survivors in a pile of rubble intended to mimic a disaster scene—and Vara has found her live person.

All the dogs of the *V* litter have been in odor training now for weeks. Odor training is not training to notice odors; all dogs do that naturally. It is training them to think about that one odor that we care about—and to tell us when they have found it. The working dogs in training are first exposed to a new scent: universal detector calibrant, or UDC. In large quantities UDC smells to the human nose like "sawdust and cleaning supplies," according to Amritha's human nose. The compound was designed to be unlike odors one typically comes across in daily life, as well as stable at different temperatures, safe to handle, and detectable by nose. Using this odor allows the trainers to teach the dogs to search before they are committed to their "career" odor, be it narcotics, missing persons, or the smell of disease.

The dogs first meet the smell when taken to a specially designed room. It is empty but for a few elbow pipes set on the floor; other pipes are set into a plywood wall like portholes. In one of these pipes a very small amount of UDC is hidden. Harnessing the power of puppy curiosity, trainers simply let the dogs explore the room. When a pup happens, after a few seconds or many minutes, to poke their nose near the UDC-smelling pipe, the trainer sounds a clicker, and, thrillingly, a dog treat is spontaneously tossed onto the floor near them. The dog is led away after eating the treat and then released again—so of course they go looking for more treats. When they happen across the odor again, click, treat. Their recognition of the game being played here is almost visible on their faces: soon they strategize, trying the same *place*, the same *behavior*... until they get it—the same *smell*.

From this first exposure the *V* litter has graduated into practicing finding an odor in larger rooms and on a custom-designed scent wheel—a merry-go-round with odor-containing glass jars where the cars would be. And now they are in training outside, too, searching for other smells, like one likely to be found in the world—person smell—but unlikely in the environment of a pile of rubble or a big field. When they detect the scent, they are encouraged to bark as their way of notifying their handlers that they have found whatever the thing is to be found. Not to bark once, or a few times, but a dozen times. Or two dozen. The *V* litter dogs are larger than Quid, but their barks are surprisingly similar: piercing, excitement verging on desperation. Every one of them excels at the bark alert.

In a parallel universe, where everything is identical but for our urgent need of a skilled locator of and alerter to squirrels, small dogs, and passing cars, Quid would be a hero. I feel a little sympathy for her that she, so clearly a master bark alerter, was destined to live in a family in which that skill would not be celebrated.

Barks, whines, and growls aside, most of dogs' talk is with actions. None of these action words has been taught to her. A paw on my hand: a request to keep petting her. Turning her head away: a refusal, expression of distaste or disgust. Head resting on my lap: somewhere between possession and affection.

It takes *years of life* for humans, who are explicitly taught and genetically predisposed to learn language, to understand a reference like *look at that bird*. Yet with puppies, we say no to their barks and expect that they will understand our meaning immediately.

JULY ❀ 6 MONTHS
To Sleep, Perchance

Right now a puppy naps beside me. Quid is melted onto a cushion, her legs and tail outstretched. Her top ear lies inside out. She twitches her toes, and her tail thumps a beat on the cushion. No doubt she is dreaming of the five-mile hike we've just had.

She is nearly six months old. Spring has turned into deep summer. On the porch with me, she hops up to sit on my lap as I write, watching the tiny twitches of my pencil until her ears alert her to a distant dog bark, a barred owl hoot. Her attentive gaze—eyes, ears, and nose—tracks a woodpecker's hammering in a tree, then a quarrel with a nuthatch. The top of her head smells like the air above a river, that fresh, clean smell of water and energy. She *is* that energy, a rush of river and air made flesh.

She is homing in on her style. It includes the dreaded barking—at a passing runner or trotting dog. Despite her shrill greeting, she plays well with others; she seems happy to play with puppies; with tall, large dogs; with old dogs. She learns that squirrels disappear into trees, bringing her awareness to a whole nother dimension: up. She jumps after their disappearing tails, surprising herself, and one day she discovers that she can launch herself up the stairs in explosive bunny hops. Our upstairs hideout is rendered useless. *Down* is another thing entirely. To go down she tumbles, letting her legs scatter forth, marbles let loose down the stairs. For the dogs we have placed carpets as traction on each landing, concession to their aging limbs. The stairs remind us all of our bodies.

Finn lies aside me, shooting me occasional looks. He has been my dearest companion for so long, I can read his tenseness at this trespasser. Once in a while he stalks her on the path to the house and swipes at her with his mouth as she tries to run by. That's fair, I think. He has been slowing down. His back legs are uncoordinated; he exhausts more quickly. Sometimes he stumbles; sometimes I find him marooned, standing with his back feet together, a tripod. He is easily knocked down by an overenthusiastic puppy. His face has gotten leaner, and his eyes have lost their luster. Even as Quid's tail is winding up, Finn's has lost its vibrancy.

Each dog reflects a part of me, I think. I see in Finn the responsible one, always the good student, following rules; in Upton the clownish character, a pleasure in being silly. I don't see myself in Quid yet. Must I? Is that part of coming to love her?

I do love her *asleep*. Just gazing at a sleeping dog relaxes me. Oh, the many satisfactions and ways she sleeps! On Ogden's lap in the car on the way back from walks; on my lap in the evening after the final play zoomabouts with the dogs; on, by, or under a dog or cat. Earlier, after a run, she conked out on my feet as I stood at the sink washing dishes.

🦴

I could say that my fondness for seeing a sleeping puppy comes from knowing about the cognitive growth that happens in sleep. Despite the seeming lack of activity on the outside, there is a firestorm happening in the brain during sleep. In humans it is a time of memory and learning consolidation: memories are strengthened; things learned during the day are solidified. Getting REM, the dreamy rapid eye movement sleep, is important for emotional regulation and interpretation, as well as for creativity. The rest of the body benefits, too. Sleep helps maintain a healthy immune system, normal metabolism, and even cardiovascular fitness.

Dogs' ancestors, wolves, are for the most part nocturnal, active at night. Under the cover of night is a good time to hunt (and evade predators). Dogs have adjusted—or been adjusted, through domestication—to our non-nocturnal human schedule and are mostly active during the daytime. This is not to say that they never sleep during the day. Adult dogs might sleep for up to a quarter of the daylight hours (and three-quarters of nighttime hours)—more, if they are given nothing to do during the day. Young puppies, and even six-month-old puppies, sleep much longer during the day than they will as young adults.

It is not a coincidence that most of Quid's sleep is on or near us. In one survey of dog sleeping behavior, researchers found that if allowed to, 87 percent of dogs choose to sleep close to a person. (Well over half of people forbid their dogs to sleep near them, though.) For us, letting Quid sleep in Ogden's bedroom allowed her—and us—to sleep through the night; one wonders how many similarly simple fixes of behavior could be enabled by just changing the rules around where a dog sleeps.

On the other hand, all that healthy brain- and body-developing sleep not only gives full rein to her proper development, it permits her more difficult behaviors to thrive. Ah, well, a risk we have to take.

Exactly how sleep helps learning in dogs has not been as well researched as it has with people. In 2020, the researchers in my lab and I took advantage of all the people at home full-time with their pups and recruited subjects for an experiment to test this. We asked volunteers to teach their dogs to touch—to touch their nose to their person's open palm on cue. The clever trainer Victoria Stilwell, who provided our human subjects with a step-by-step training video, uses touch as a way to scaffold more-complicated requests. Once you have a dog moving to get their nose to your palm, for instance, your palm becomes an attractant, and you can move your dog around—off the bed, onto a perch—by just asking them to touch it.

Our canine subjects were divided into two groups: one learned "touch" in the evening, one in the morning. Then each group of people tested their dog's performance twelve hours later—after a night of sleep or a day of (mostly) awakeness. Every pup learned the trick, and both subject groups performed pretty well when tested again. But the pups who had slept before their test were both faster and better at the task than the daytime group. Of the daytime group, those who napped more during the day were better than the light nappers. As with most of the science from our lab, what we find translates into an immediate change in how I think about the dogs in my home. After learning this, we have shifted the training we do to the evening—to be followed by a long night's sleep, so that they awaken ready to "touch," "sit," and "come." And I now monitor my sleeping pup not only for suckling and running in her dreams, but for dream nose bumping.

It turns out that Quid is actually the biggest sleeper of her litter. I was curious to hear more of the pups' stories a half year into their lives. I have seen that the eleven Maize puppies have developed their own ear, nohawk, and eye styles, but what about their personalities? There is no science that links the genes for scruffiness to mischievousness per se. But much is made of the influence of dogs' genes on their personalities: breed standards for purebred dogs are founded on the idea that, given a known set of parents, their young will be in many ways predictable not just in their appearance but also in their temperament: bold, friendly, fearless, and so on.

I send everyone a survey asking about their habits, their pup's behaviors—and also asking for three words they think best describe their puppy's personality. For Quid I list *rambunctious*, *playful*, *clever* (sometimes too clever by half). Several other pups are also described as *smart*, a number of others as *energetic*—if not of the rambunctious variety. *Affectionate* or *loving*—even *all-loving*—appear in several responses, as well as *cuddly* (definitely not Quid). One pup is *thoughtful*, another *kind*, and another *gentle*. These are not *full* siblings, surely . . .

Few of the other puppies' people describe any problems with

barking—although, to be fair, most of them did say that their dogs bark at delivery persons or new people and dogs. They just do not see it as a problem. Two dogs—presumably the kind and thoughtful ones—*never bark*. I stare at those answers a long time, envying them. Five pups are described as shy or fearful when meeting new people or dogs, and whine or hide behind their person—now unimaginable for Quid. Ten of eleven pups love to chase birds and squirrels. A handful chase their tails. All but Quid, apparently, are described by their people as snugglers.

The most satisfying portion of the survey is what people say are their favorite things about these dogs. "Everything," one person replies. Another: "I wouldn't change a thing."

The biggest tell of the pups' relatedness—or of their pandemic lifestyle—comes with the question, "Does your dog generally follow you from room to room?" Unanimity. Eleven pups, scattered out in different parts of the northeastern United States, dutifully keeping at the heels of their person from kitchen to bathroom to bed.

PART 3

QUID YEARS

AUGUST ❀ 7 MONTHS
Gale Force Ten

I sit on the living room floor with my legs out, my book resting on my lap while I watch her. The air is late-summer hot; the dogs lie on their sides, legs extended midtrot on an invisible wall. Quid rises and moves to the soft dog bed in the corner. She curls in its curve, stays twenty seconds, and rises again. She tries lying right at Finnegan's rump, her head resting over his back feet. Nope. Up again, to the dog bed, which is really Finnegan's. A short stay. She approaches me and plops down perpendicular to me, close enough to rest her head on my knee. Nope. Finally, she heads under the dining room table and flops on her side, squeezing herself between the table legs. That's the one.

The puppy is in heat: her reproductive cycle has started, and her body is fertile and able to breed. Finnegan is the one to tell us about it. He has been playing with her incessantly. That is odd: their play is occasional at best—and usually after dinner, when their leftover excitement about a good meal is redirected toward each other. The next day Finn is her shadow, regularly gnawing on her back in his corncobby way. It is nice to see him rejuvenated, but it is clearly her smell doing the rejuvenating. Though he was neutered when we met him fourteen years ago, a neutered dog can still smell—and desire—sex. Quid is more interested in her own nether regions than usual, too.

Given the science showing the importance of hormones in early bone, brain, and muscle growth, Quiddity will go through a heat cycle or two before being spayed. Our vet is on board; Dr. Cindy Otto, director of the Working Dog Center, tells me they do not spay their females until fourteen months; renowned vet Dr. Karen Becker advocates waiting until three to four years for a routine spay—but, short of that, recommends simply waiting "as long as possible . . . Every month adds beneficial hormone secretions that will serve her well later." All we have to do is keep her from any unneutered males, which is completely doable with some attention (and a leash). Happily, Quid is mostly on leash already, because of her overenthusiastic interest in squirrels, so there is no change there.

Her heat lasts three weeks. I mark its length by how keen the dogs are on her in the morning and evening. Evenings are a big riot, with Finn and, more recently, Upton nibbling her and angling for her body. I tell Ogden that this is a preview of his life in a couple of years, with some boys skulking around trying to get some girl's attention, and her going hot and cold with the boys. It does feel recognizably teenagerish.

⤬

We don't know Maize's life history, but we do know that about sixty days before she arrived in upstate New York, she had an encounter with a boy dog.

And we know that somehow Maize found a fella she could put up with for the several necessary minutes of intercourse. He more likely found her, as male dogs some distance away are able to pick up the scent of a female in heat, detecting the change wrought by her rising levels of estrogen. While anecdotal reports describe males coming from miles around to find a female in heat, exactly how far away they can detect the odors in her urine hasn't been scientifically investigated, surprisingly. Maize possibly consorted with more than one male: a litter can include pups who have different fathers. All we know is, two months later she was in upstate New York and something big was happening in her belly.

Over the last few decades, breeding has changed significantly for dogs—at least, for some dogs. While it is easy enough for dogs to find one another and mate if left to their own devices, breeders of purebred dogs would rather not leave it to their devices. A champion dog's choice of mate would likely not be the same choice that a breeder, with the breed's desired features in mind, would make. Purebred dogs' sex lives are arranged: matching good or desirable genes, or good looks or temperament, with same. Many of these arranged purebred matches happen without the dogs ever getting within sniffing distance of each other. Only their sperm and eggs ever meet.

🦴

Outside, summer fades to fall. Smells rise from the ground in layers, warmed by the morning sun. I am running with Quid. We have had maybe a dozen runs together thus far. She has been surprisingly good: just running ahead of me on the park path, in pursuit of some real or imagined small animal, then, once they fly off or disappear in the brush, turning back around to wait for me to catch up. But then the invisible rubber band between us begins getting stretched too taut. She is racing farther and farther away in her headstrong pursuit of a bird or bunny—either unaware of where I am or perfectly aware but just comfortable with it.

I am less comfortable with it. She might run off, get lost, harass animals or people. So I begin taking her on leash for the runs. At first she deals with it by circling me and stepping directly in front of me. Now she just mildly zigzags but is still pulling hard, a little sled dog with an unwilling load.

Today, as she pulls suddenly at the sight of a rabbit, I let out a yelp. I hear it come out of me like an exhale, involuntarily. At the noise Quid is instantly alarmed. Her ears flatten on her head, and she stops, looks back at me, and hurries to my side. Whether out of concern or through thinking my yelp was directed at her, it has the effect of reining her in.

The next time she pulls, I give a little yelp experimentally— almost a quote of my previous one: *Yelp?* Quid immediately slows and moves alongside me. And again, another time. Within a few minutes she is jogging by my side, looking up at me with a smile (of her eyes and tail), matching my pace—and continues to, without leash or yelp. Four bunnies cross our path; she pulls to not a one. It feels miraculous. She clearly could do this behavior all along; we just never asked her to in a way she understood. Whether my yelping feels to me like a polite way to ask or not, it conveys the message to her.

She's changing. She is more sensitive. She begins to startle at perfectly normal things. A container of laundry soap on the floor prompts ferocious barking. Even after a peaceful introduction to the bottle on its side, she remains unconvinced that it is not a threat. The vacuum, which she formerly followed around like a duckling with her duck mom, suddenly concerns her.

At the same time, she is even more headstrong and more vigilant at home. She watches the activities of the house with both ears, her right ear turned back to catch what is happening in the kitchen, her left ear toward me, across the room, and her eyes on the dogs in front of her. When the cat sidles up to her and starts licking, Quid snaps at her and walks away. Her previously magical ability to wait at the door before going in or out has turned into a new trick: I ask her to wait, and she runs by, ignoring me. Many mornings I call her name, she looks right at me, and she trots the other way. I can almost hear her slamming her bedroom door behind her.

The dog park, once a place of much joy, turns sour. She has changed, or the community of dogs has changed, for on entrance this time she is targeted by a dog with a certain surly gleam in her eye. Every time Quid makes a gesture toward running, the surly dog runs up to and over her, nipping. Quid shrieks, a new sound, and tries repeatedly to get back over to me. With a storm approaching and a darkening sky settling over us, Quid nearly leaps the fence trying to get out. We hustle home, just making it before the clouds empty themselves.

We are inside. I look at Quid, still holding a stick she carried back from the dog park. Maybe it is the charge in the air, but her fur looks electrified. The scruff around her ears and snout is longer; the hair on the back of her legs points backward. Her tail looks as if it were snatched from a red fox; it has blossomed into bushiness. I feel a wash of pleasure to know her, even realizing how little I do know about her, how she is changing right before my eyes. She is looking back at me expectantly, so I do what she expects: I tickle her ears, gently ask for the stick, and we head down the hall to find her a treat.

🦴

Adolescence unites fruit flies, lobsters, zebras, and humans—only the duration of adolescence for the fly is about five days, whereas in humans it is about seven years (between the ages of ten and seventeen). Quid has entered this golden age—thought to be, for dogs, from approximately six months old (varying by breed) through their second birthday. Just when we thought we were done with sensitive periods of development, another one races in—only this one is woefully understudied by researchers and often completely ignored by dog people.

But there is good reason to pay heed to this period in their life. As is widely acknowledged in humans, adolescence is a distinct stage of development: one is no longer a child but far from an adult. It is a time of risk-taking, social and sexual experimentation, and roller-coaster emotions. No one looks at a fourteen-year-old boy's oddly distant yet needy behavior, his increasing independence and quarrelsomeness, and wonders what bit him. We know what bit him: he is a teenager. When we look at an adolescent dog suddenly refusing to come when called, seemingly willfully misbehaving, though, people are more disposed to think *Oh, they're a bad dog* than *Oh, they're going through a phase.* We acknowledge puppyhood in dogs, then race them into adulthood, but there is in fact a long transition getting from cute pup to mature adult. A primary reason for abandoning dogs in shelters is behavioral—they jump, bite, escape, soil the house. They are aggressive to animals; they are aggressive to people; they destroy things. And there is a severe uptick in dogs being given up during adolescence, partly due to the uptick in these behaviors. Since many unadopted dogs are still euthanized, or put to death, "simply being an adolescent can count as a fatal condition," write the authors of a book about adolescence, *Wildhood.*

Puberty can mark the beginning of adolescence. Quid's pubertal heat is the start: it is the time in her reproductive cycle when her estrogen levels rise; she then moves through several stages, similar to those of the human cycle. It not only marks the occasion of her being able to become pregnant; it is also the beginning of a period of rapid growth. Dogs jump from half to nearly all their final weight from puppyhood to late adolescence—a little earlier in small and toy breeds, a little later in giant breeds. They reach nearly their final height at the shoulder by seven months. The increase in hormones also leads to increased sensitivities and less self-control. These hormones affect every system of the body—and incidentally, they are basically the same hormones in people as in anteaters, otters, and dogs. Adolescence also oversees a rewiring of the brain—especially, in mammals, in the areas that regulate emotions and make judgments. The result is a changed mind and body; along the way, there can be turbulence. "Like waking up in your tent in the wilderness, in a gale force ten," as trainer Sarah Fisher put it—both for the pups and for their people.

This time is not quite as sensitive a sensitive period as the previous one, but it is still a significant time in dogs' early lives. They are still developing, and what happens now can affect their later behavior. Research has connected events and living situations of early adolescence with various personality traits and behaviors as young adults. For instance, being isolated (in a kennel or left alone outdoors) or injured (through punishment or attack) during this period has been connected to later problems in interacting with other dogs or people. Dogs who have been threatened or attacked by an unknown dog as adolescents are significantly more likely to be fearful or aggressive toward dogs as young adults. At least in research with rats, having an enriched environment in adolescence completely undoes the negative effects of the early-life stressor of being separated from their mothers—such as might be experienced by a dog from a puppy mill or other adverse life beginning.

Getting through dog adolescence involves some bumps. What is called, flatly, disobedience seems to rise during this time.

Part of the reason for this is that puppyhood involves learning, to some degree, what the rules of the house are; being trained, to whatever degree, to sit or come or shake a paw when asked. There is a license granted to puppies to get things wrong now and then. As they grow, the expectations for their performance grow faster than they do. Plus, hormones. Just as one might expect an adolescent human child to possibly not "come here" when called, one research study found that dogs who learned to sit on command as puppies are less likely to do it as adolescents—and are more likely to sit when a stranger, not their person (think: parent) asks. An adolescent dog is trying to expand their world, to become more adult—hence the seeming challenging of their person's authority. Pups starting this growth spurt might become sensitive to touch, alternating shying from you and clinging to you; they may start climbing or jumping on people or things. As dogs explore the world partly with their mouths, there might be more chewing of undesired objects as well as licking. This might read as misbehavior, but in some cases it may actually be a way of self-medicating: chewing, for instance, may help lower stress-hormone levels. Quid's sudden stick obsession falls squarely in this territory, as does her changing interaction with older dogs, now that she can't get away with being that cute puppy they all humored.

As so often during early life with dogs, patience is due. Providing an acceptable outlet for their chewing, licking, climbing—as well as some time without demands—is recommended for a safe journey through adolescence.

While paying so much attention to trying to get Quid to run with me, I almost overlook her *runningness*. It is masterful. She has developed in seven months into the fastest runner in our family by leaps and bounds (and partially via leaping and bounding).

The sheer physical aptitude and grace of dogs running at full throttle is satisfying to watch. Despite the fact that dogs are literally on their tiptoes all the time—the design of their legs is such that their heels never touch the ground—their balance is impeccable from the start. With Quid, I stay on the sidelines, laughing involuntarily with surprise and pleasure as she runs zoomies around another dog. The joy of it!

At the Working Dog Center, the pups have recently faced the so-called impossible task—similar to the one used to gauge whether dogs look to us for assistance. The task is essentially to open a box that is, simply, unopenable without tools. Or not: "A couple of our dogs have broken into the impossible task box," Dana admits. These pups from past litters have found a way to wedge their teeth into it and crack it. The researchers have had to up their box security twice. Now the box is essentially a thick wooden structure with a sealable well in its belly in which a toy can be stashed.

At just over six months old, the *V* litter meets the box. A video recorder is trained on Vauk, excited to be in this room with her trainers, excited to see what's next. Dana pulls out an orange ball—the ball of many young pups' dreams—attached to a short rope, while a second trainer holds Vauk by her harness a few feet away. The pup is thrilled. She begins barking brightly, straining at the harness to get to the ball. Dana slips it in the well in the box and sits down. When released, Vauk beelines for it and pulls the ball out by the rope with a soft touch. The trainers erupt in congratulations. As Vauk prances about with her prize, they additionally reward her with a short game of tug. Then they take the ball back, and the whole scenario is repeated several times, with a Plexiglas lid placed a bit more over the well each time. On the fifth go Dana *screws* the lid over the well, and Vauk is released to find her ball. She runs with enthusiasm, mouths the lid, steps back with surprise, and barks. And barks and barks. She tries mouthing the lid again, but it is like a Frisbee glued to the ground: she can get her mouth on it, nearly around it, but it is immovable. She resorts to frantic digging of the box; in her efforts she circles around it seventeen times, as though trying to unscrew the lid with her body. More barking, more mouthing, more digging. It is the nightmarish behavior of any pet left at home alone who decides they must get that ball under the couch . . . and proceeds to chew through the couch until they reach it. But for Vauk, who continues trying to get into the box for the full five minutes allotted, it is a brilliant success. She is wildly persistent, never appealing to the two humans in the room to *just help her out a little bit*. In the end Dana unscrews the lid for her, and Vauk pulls the ball out with glee. She is on her way to being an excellent working dog.

Six of the eight pups persevere for the full five minutes. This time, none gets in—but then, that was never the point of the test. Instead, it is a gauge of their persistence behaviors—which are impressive. They date back to the puppies' strong start pursuing toys and noises and getting all the praise for it. In a home, their behavior would be misbehavior, but here it is celebrated. Watching Vauk get to perform all these exceedingly doggy behaviors and get rewarded, not punished, for them is a reminder of how challenging it is for puppies to comport themselves in a way suitable to human, not dog, standards of behavior. Even with her frustration at not being able to get her ball, Vauk is the happiest-looking dog I have seen in a long while—just from having been allowed to do what comes naturally to her and her species.

SEPTEMBER ❃ 8 MONTHS
Seeing Us

Quid and I have struck a deal. Every morning she flies up the stairs, leaps onto our bed, and attacks my nose with her sharp little teeth. And I am awakened.

Oh wait, no: We don't have a deal. She just does that. It is vexing and charming at once. Just at the moment of nose attack, I can smell the sleep collected on her breath and fur. It mingles with the odor of the other dogs in the room and is beginning to smell to me like home. Since her heat, she has become more interested in contact with us of any sort. She minds where we are, beating a hasty path after us if we rise from a chair to leave the room, sometimes licking our ankles as we go. She lies next to me on the couch, her body contorted to maximize body-to-body contact—somewhat at odds with the expected adolescent behavior.

Just now she is lying on my feet as I sit at my desk—her recent discovery of how to remain touching when I am perched on a chair too small for gal *and* dog. The weight of her head on my foot is peak dog-human happiness. I find it impossible to move and displace her, so when I do need to rise, I text Ammon to phone me. She lifts her head at the sound of the ring, and I make my escape.

It feels as if she has come to a different level of awareness of us.

She is seeing us; she is minding us. With this she has developed a knowing look. Picking up a peanut butter jar lid on the floor, she gently mouths it and carries it over to a dog bed, the prey captured and brought back to her den. Another day she hurries into Ogden's room, then saunters out carrying his sock, lazily mouthing it, looking right at me. There is a real understanding going on there, between my seeing her and her seeing me see her (and now my seeing her see me see her). It's an understanding of who we are, how we tend to react, and what that means for the actions she is doing at the moment. It is what causes puppies to discover that your tone of voice, when you catch them aiming their heads toward a pile of some other dog's poo in the park, will be followed by your interfering—so they hurry up and grab a mouthful and run.

Quid now reveals some awareness that I am attached to the same leash she is. She has learned *go around* in the inevitable situations that arise with long leashes and trees in forests. Like all the dogs, she stares wide-eyed at me while she poos. *Yeah? I'm doing this right now*, their gazes seem to say. Given the disgust she shows for her own poo, she must think me dangerous, dense, or equipped with smell-deflecting superpowers.

With her heightened attention to us, she knows right when we are about to leave the house. There is a reason she keeps her head on my foot: that way the foot can't walk me out the door. She has learned that we now might leave. It is reasonable that she might have thought otherwise. We have been with her continually since birth. If one of us left, another stayed; there was no occasion on which we all had to leave. With the coming of fall, and the loosening of restrictions in response to the pandemic's waning, this changes: we leave the house. Without her. To acclimate her, we practice leaving—almost as much for us as for her. We all step out of the house together, go on an aimless five-minute walk, then step back in without fuss. Then we step out for twenty minutes. Then for an hour. And then we drive off in a car, only returning two hours later. She seems to handle separation from us well, in that on our return, the house is an intact structure not held together with dog urine and tiny bits of couch stuffing. But she greets us with a new desperation, wiggling so hard the energy comes out of her mouth in the form of a continual cry.

Observing us, she has done a decent job of training us. If I presume to stop tickling her belly before she deems it time to stop, she looks at me with great seriousness of purpose, then paws me, requesting more tickles. As I sit on the couch one day responding to my mistress's every demand for tickles, the cat slowly wanders between us. I stop tickling, and Quid, per her wont, tries to paw me—pawing the cat instead. Edsel responds by calmly but firmly biting her on that paw. Quid looks completely surprised. She paws again. The cat bites again, more forcefully this time. Quid looks at her and tries again. The cat bites with vehemence and a yowl that communicates even to the unschooled. Not only do I suddenly see how much more trainable I am than the cat, I realize that though I thought Quid had learned to touch me to make a request, what she has really learned is something slightly different: to *stretch your leg out* when you want something. The communication was not the touch; it was the feeling inside her when her leg moved— whether there is a cat in the way or not. As surprised as the cat is, Quid is no less surprised to learn that she is saying something she didn't know she was saying. What I assumed to be communication was really the result of happening to be nearby when she stretched her leg.

Puppy attempts to communicate with the cat

When I was writing my first book on dog cognition, I asked my friend Daniel what he would like to know about a dog's mind. At the time, he lived with Maggie, a good-natured mixed breed with fetching eyebrows and a fearsome wag. "What does she know about me?" he said. His response has stayed with me, as it is not uncommon. People wonder not just what their dogs are thinking, but what they are thinking about them—whether they know our secrets, harbor any ill will; whether they see through our deceits or feel the love we feel for them. My answer then, and now, is usually the same: science is pretty quiet on the matter. But to be sure, they are thinking about us, and it is striking to be held in their gaze. We adopted a puppy, not thinking that she would see us so well.

୧୬

Dogs' knowing anything at all about us begins with our taking them in—began with our domesticating of them thousands of years ago—and is extended by their tendency to care about our faces. Not only are they very good at looking at our faces, as we have seen; they are also skilled at using those faces to get information about the minds behind them.

As we greet our dogs, sharing a long gaze, we are tuned to see some recognition there. Their faces match ours mainly in the particulars—the somewhat-frontal eyes, the prominent nose and mouth. Dogs also have a particular facial muscle that enables them to raise their inner eyebrows in an appealing way that is deeply familiar to humans: we do it, too.

When looking at our faces, dogs appear to see more than just an array of parts. They seem to understand that our eyes—and our gazes—hold meaning. Gazes relay emotion, convey attention, and impart information. At less than a year old, Quid can follow my gaze to find the food I have dropped, to quickly understand if I am about to head toward my sneakers or my chair—to know what I know, in a way.

By thinking about what we know, dogs become skilled at some very humanlike guile. One study found that dogs forbidden to eat a treat are pretty good at following those directions when a person is in the room with them but steal treats right away if the lights are turned off (notably, dogs' night vision is exceptional, unlike ours); they are a little less likely to steal any treats if a spotlight is directed at the treat in an otherwise dark room. So they seem to be basing their theft on whether the person in the room with them can see them or the treat. It is important to mention that in every situation most subjects stole at least some treats, so their cognition is tuned to treats at least as much as to *What does that person see?* If the person leaves the room, forget it: most dogs studied in the various experiments that have asked them to obey even in the person's absence just go right ahead and disobey as soon as the person is gone. Out of room, out of mind. When the person comes back into the room after this disobedience, the dog might react guiltily—ducking their head, looking away, frantically wagging low between their legs—but this reaction is not an indication of their guilt at disobedience but of their sensitivity to whether we think they are guilty. For they show more of this guilty look when their person thinks they have eaten the treat—whether or not they have—than when the person thinks they haven't. Again, dogs read our minds—and in this case, our unconscious body language.

There are, we now know, many things that dogs know about us that we ourselves do not, of course. In particular, dogs have been trained to detect various cancers, to notice low blood sugar levels or imminent seizures. The very first reported cases of dogs detecting cancers—a dachshund puppy who noticed a breast cancer and a Labrador who found a melanoma—happened with untrained dogs. In both cases the dogs were simply persistently sniffing at a part of their person's body (left armpit, left thigh); months later, their people realized the dogs might be onto something and went to their physicians. (This is not to say that your dog is an early-detection system for such diseases—but if my dogs were suddenly and doggedly keen on sniffing my big toe, I would probably check it out.) Within months of the novel coronavirus's spread, dogs were being trained to detect the virus in people who themselves did not yet know if they had contracted it. Would Quid know? We got a chance to find out when first Ammon, then I, came down with the virus. There was no sign that Quid sniffed it out—or, at least, we did not notice her trying to tell us. And that's the trick: as interested as people profess to be in what their dogs know about them, we aren't often listening to what they might be saying.

Beliefs and knowledge of an eight-month-old puppy

* The exact distance to wait outside the kitchen in order to get an occasional glimpse and toss of dinner prep from the chef.

* Where everyone is in the morning, should you need to boop them on the mouth (which you do).

* That both inside and outside are "the place on the other side of that door," in the question *Do you want to go inside/outside?*

* Outside is for peeing.

* If you continue to squirm on your back on the bed, you will eventually fall right off the bed (still: worth it).

* It's four turns, past the swallow field, past the straight-away with rabbits, next to the field with the giant birds, past the stream, past the second stream, before the curve, to meet up with the rest of the family.

* The window upstairs to look out of to see who's outside, if you can't see them out of the first or second window you try.

* The pleasure of catching one's own tail.

* If you stay still near the door, you might get a halter put over your head. But you also get a small nugget of something tasty.

* If you feel unsafe, first try to get on the large person's lap. If you determine that the lap is not available, between her legs will do.

* When the door opens, run as fast as you can, keeping alert, and a squirrel will manifest to be chased.

* If another small dog yaps at you, the proper response is to yap back, louder.

* To get out of the building to the place with all the pigeons, with the ground spread with smells, you first need to enter a small room and stand still. There is nothing else you do in that room: there are no toys, there is no food, and there is no soft place to lie down. It makes a kind of hum, sometimes jostles, and then beeps. At the beep, look pensively at the people, and they will open the door for you to leave.

* It doesn't look like it at first, but the steep cliffs in the house can be leaped to the top of. You may find another cliff there! Just leap that one too, and the next—eventually, there is flatness again.

* You can make the gate open by looking at people (first choice) or vigorous touching with paws (if they don't look *right away*).

* Where the soft spaces in the house are.

* Where the warm spaces in the house are.

* Secret spaces where you might find the cat.

* Before settling down someplace, it's useful to dig frantically into the surface to make it nice for settling into.

OCTOBER ❦ 9 MONTHS
The Thing About Sleds

It snows all night, the sky unrelenting in its release. In the morning the air is crisp and the snow is high. The landscape is primed for navigation by sled. We unbury two long plastic models, and Quid follows us up and down gamely—showing pleasure and confusion with our shape-shifting. Then she decides that sledding is about being very fast. And as we stop and turn to mount the hill again, she continues running very fast, past the edge of the driveway, through snow six inches higher than she is tall, until she catches wind of a trio of deer and disappears after them. We drop the sleds and run, too, calling her name into the bright morning.

Finnegan can no longer keep up with the sleds, and the slipperiness of hard-packed snow is tricky as he loses balance and strength. He was our initiator into the pleasure and terror of sledding with dogs: he was very sure that the sledder must be caught, must be brought to a stop. He would race after us, mouth wide in a smile, barking and nibbling at our coat sleeves, until we crashed and he could come attack us properly. Quid is no Finn. Her understanding of sledding is less about us and more about speed.

We catch up with Quid well past the neighbor's house and carry her home, knowing we cannot impart to her how disappointing it is that she flees. So now I walk in the forest with her on leash, wishing that she could be off leash without running from me. But we are beginning to see her for who she is. She is tuned to outside, to the world buzzing around her. Her body is tense and alert; her ears are erect. She tracks invisible paths underfoot; she stops to sniff the most ordinary fallen branch for a full 197 seconds. (I counted.) She is in the forest in a way that I have never been in the forest: as though new to the world, receiving all its news at once.

Yet here I am struggling with her pulling on the leash. I realize that we have not followed trainers' counsel to always have great treats with us, in order to make ourselves "the most interesting thing" to her. We may have neglected to have treats on our person all the time; we may have all been irregular in our treating of her; we may have let her strain at the leash when we should not have—whatever it is, we are not excelling.

But as I contend with her willfulness, I see a great, obvious truth: we simply aren't the most interesting thing out here. There are the loping deer! Darting squirrels and chipmunks! Smells of dogs, birds, coyotes, and raccoons who have passed by. As much as I would like Quid to have what the trainers call a bombproof recall—quickly and agreeably coming whenever I call for her—I see no reason to endorse and then perpetuate the myth that we are the most interesting things around. We're not. I mean, I am perfectly decent company, should you meet me and never have had anyone to ask all those questions about your dog. But I am not singularly interesting—more interesting *than anything else*. My goodness.

And also thank goodness! I do want Quid to be interested in us, in coming when we request it—for her sake, for our sake, and for the sake of anyone else around—but imagine if she never left our side. We have to shower and leave the house and be by ourselves without her world ending. And she has to be a dog, to be herself: indeed, this is the very reason we wanted to know her. What I want is to be "somewhat to moderately interesting" to my dog, and my big plan to get there does not involve always smelling of salmon treats.

I appreciate Quid's calling my attention to the chipmunks living in the stone wall and the rivulet of water across the path, her reminding me to notice the funky, fragrant smells in the middle of a forest. A breeze hits us, and Quid angles her nose upward, nostrils working to pull in the air. She noisily exhales, jowls flapping *puhbapuhba*. Walking with the dogs in the forest is keeping their company, but they are also our guides to the animals that have been there before. Here is where a brace of deer slept last night; this is where a squirrel dug up a cherished acorn; this spot, the intersection of two invisible highways, is where the local coyote leaves messages in fur and pee. As she tugs at the leash, Quid is telling me that it is I who insisted she wear the silly thing—and that she has been pretty good-natured about it, given how nonsensical it is in her world.

The trainer Sophia Yin once wrote that "whether we're aware of it or not, every interaction we have with the pet is a training session." For *training* read *learning*, and I might add that it is training for me as well. I've learned something new about the puppy: she has a different pace than we do. It is not just that she moves quickly. Her speed and growth are indicative of existing at her own tempo, one in which moments are not long and idle, as with our older dogs, but full of minutiae and anticipation.

Our walks with all the dogs have become comic, my arms pulled in three directions as Upton stands his ground, nose in the air; Finn limpingly greets each stranger passing by; and Quiddity trembles with excitement to dart at every-dog-every-pigeon-every-person-what-is-that. At last we figure out we should take the dogs on independent walks. We fence in a section of forest behind the house, creating a subforest within the forest where Quid can pursue her pace. I rake the generations of fallen leaves to make several serpentine, intersecting paths. Within this area she is free to explore as she wants: she need not stay on path; she is not tethered to us; we are not going directly from point A to point B in the way that humans (but not dogs) walk. She takes to it immediately, or maybe it is just what the world would look like if mapped to her. She runs madly along the paths. She minds the perimeter. She noses each hole that appears in the ground.

One day I bring an old tennis ball out to her fenced forest and toss it. With that toss Quid found her raison d'être. Her reason for being is to get that ball, to bring it back, and to get the next ball. We had no idea that hidden within this scruffy, long-eared pup there was a ball obsessive. Just as there are dog dogs and people dogs, ball dogs are a devout class. They may have very specific ideas about type of ball, age of ball, color and size of ball, desirable level of filthiness of ball, squeakiness or squishability of ball, and ownership of ball (with, at times, other dogs' balls being the best balls). Quid turns out to be a *type: tennis ball; preference: slightly squishy* ball dog. I have never lived with a committed ball dog. I have a lot to learn.

Puppy's true love: the tennis ball

I learn first that ball dogs are not made, they are born. She was not trained on balls in her first weeks of life; she did not watch ball dogs or sleep alongside her own too-big ball. Months into her life with us, we innocently began a game indoors with a ball (type: whatever squeaks). She spontaneously retrieved the ball, working her jaw on it to make it squeak, and dropped it when I held up my hand in a fist as though I were holding a second ball—a kind of representation of ball: *Look! This is where the ball would be!* Now, outside, she simply brings it to me and drops it, stunningly. None of the retriever mixes I have known did this naturally.

I learn that she is inexhaustible. She seems to be driven by the anticipation and the chase. One could stop there, satisfied with a mouthful of fuzzy, moist, and dirt-spackled ball. But Quid has realized that the ball will go flying again if she brings it back. Dropping one at my feet, she looks at me with anticipation and focus, the only concession to anything nonball in the world being her left ear, tuned to the possibility of nearby chipmunks, just in case. We can cycle through balls until her tongue is almost completely out of her mouth. She shows no reasonableness about this: we have to stop her before she collapses.

Afterward, she lies on her side, her mouth open, panting hard, tongue pulsing on the cool floor. Her warm breath washes over my bare foot. Splatters of dirt dot her beard. I know I have about thirty minutes before she rises, gives a little shake, and is raring to go again. She is nothing like who I thought she would be. Yet this might be the pleasure of living with her. We have established a new game in the mornings after she noses me awake. I race my fingers along the bedspread, and, prone with her feet splayed behind her, she lunges after them. I drop them to the floor, and she neatly jumps down. I lift them up; she levitates. I raise them into the air, and she pauses, her hair standing on end with anticipation. I turn her in a circle with my running fingers, up-and-down her from the bed a dozen times. She whines with delight, her tail beating a brisk rhythm. As a nine-month-old puppy, she may be the most responsive person I have ever met.

🦴

If I can say that there is any difficulty involved in being a dog-cognition researcher (and really, there is not), it is simply that we can be too close to our subjects to see them well. Once we start thinking we know what we will see, we stop seeing, and the science stops. We need to not feel certain that we know what a dog means by a gesture, or what they might do next. An advantage of not knowing Quid well, even after nearly a year, is exactly that lack of closeness. I really do not know what is coming next. Watching her rise in anticipation of going out, I see her do a full-body shake. I then listen for her collar-jingling shakes for the next several weeks. I find out that, for the most part, they mark a change of activities—as from lying down to *ready to go!* Indeed, songbirds do something similar: they ruffle their feathers before going from resting to actively exploring. In both dogs and birds, the shake also likely serves as a way to release tension.

Her ears, observed closely, turn out to be revealing about her frame of mind. Their comical giantness is what started me staring at them. But whether satellite dishes or small felt triangles, each outer ear, or pinna, of a dog can move independently, enabling them to attend to both dinner making in one room and stealthy cat behavior in an adjoining room, while also picking up any outdoor squirrel, rabbit, or pigeon activity within seventy feet of the house. The pinnae are also used emotionally—something we may overlook. It is widely known that dogs will flatten their ears back along their head if feeling frustrated, worried, or fearful. But that is not the only way they use them. When, by contrast, anticipating a treat or reward, they bring their ears closer to the midline of their head. Watch for it. You will recognize the look: an earnest, hopeful face. While the topic has yet to be studied in dogs, other species with similarly mobile ears, such as sheep, show high rates of ear-posture change—going from laid back to pointed forward—when something undesirable is happening, like being separated from their flock. When they are happily feeding on fresh hay, there are fewer ear-posture changes. I sit and watch Quid watching me, her left ear kinked to the side, her right ear smoothed back against her head, and I hope that she is having the happily-feeding-on-fresh-hay feeling, too.

All the dogs benefit from the new fenced space, not just the puppy. We lay out a kind of nose-work course for Finnegan, hiding scents or treats, prompting him to find them all (which he can). Our lab's own research found that practicing nose work daily for two weeks was enough to make dogs more optimistic—a feeling an older dog may not experience much. Upton examines the far reaches of the fenced area, where the more daring local wildlife might have ducked in and left a trail (or other evidence). And Quid practices her tennis ball games.

The pleasure of having a space where a dog can be off leash is felt by both the leash holder and the held. It can be thoroughly satisfying to watch dogs run and play without human intervention—akin to the nature effect, the destressing, happy-making result of being in nature. Just as researchers in the 1980s found that watching fish in an aquarium can lower people's blood pressure and heart rate, I suspect (but know no research demonstrating) that watching dogs play does, too. For dogs, of course, being off leash enables all sorts of free exploration, vital when most of their life is controlled by people—down to where and when they get to walk, eat, poo, and socialize. More than this, though, being off leash allows dogs to have choices. Some trainers talk about *opt-in* or *opt-out* work, in which dogs are allowed to decide to participate in an activity (or not). In most situations dogs reliably opt in, even when the activity is nail clipping, as long as it is made rewarding. Giving them an option to opt out is giving dogs the chance to have a tiny bit of control over their lives. Even the best-trained dogs are also encouraged to make some choices independently. Guide dogs, for instance, are asked to do what is called intelligent disobedience: choosing to disobey their person if they see that it is not safe to obey them—such as if they see a car going through a red light. Being trusted enough to make good choices for someone else is a high level of understanding, but even for the un- or undertrained pet dog, being allowed to make choices improves their lives. I open the gate of the fence and let Quid choose what to do.

Ear Semaphore Code

Alertness

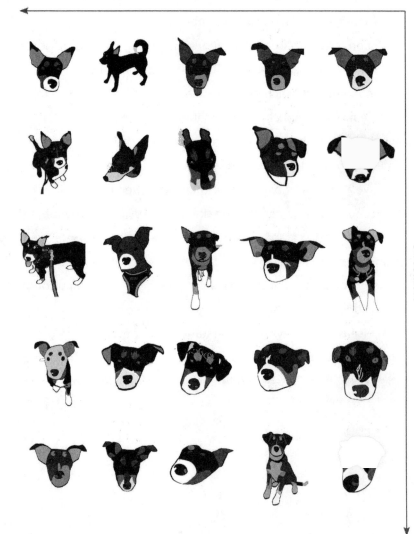

Sweetness

Illustration by Ogden Horowitz Shea

NOVEMBER ❀ 10 MONTHS
Face-First

We awaken to the aftermath of a late-season hurricane that just brushed past us: trees are deconstructed, their limbs torn; branches and leaves are scattered on every surface. For the dogs it is a universe to be explored by nose. Each leaf is examined with care.

For Quid the world has been transformed with her in mind. They are not fallen trees; it is a world made of sticks. And each stick cannot only be admired—it can be possessed! Carried right away—until we immediately come across another stick, which should also be carried. She is burdened with her choices: Which stick to carry—the one in the mouth or the one on the ground? Is it possible to carry both sticks? And what about that third stick over there? It is a physics lesson and a math lesson all at once.

She finally seems to settle on a beautiful broken birch branch, its bark peeling and mottled with lichen. But as she walks off with it, she promptly drops it at the side of the path. Soon she grabs another, wider in her mouth than she is long, and trots a bit until carefully placing it in what I must assume is its correct place. I see what she is doing: she is redecorating the forest one stick at a time.

Quid wears everything she encounters on her beard—tree debris, the mud, the pollen from the grasses, the river algae, the snow—reminding me how much of what she does is face-first. To see where that chipmunk went in the tree hollow, one does not just *gaze*, eyeballs a safe distance from the hole; one *dives in*. The leaf pile, the dirt pile—for dogs, perception is wrapped up with action. One might stick a nose right up into another dog's scruff. Their personal space in greeting is not an arm's length away but full-body contact.

Quid looking for the perfect place for that stick

Their whole experience of life is defined by contact. So many of Quid's encounters with the world are *touching* the world: rolling on the bed gleefully, using her paws to nudge a ball along while one is in her mouth, play punctuated by biting and full-body blows. In rest she settles her head on a nearby foot or hand; she stretches her body to align with ours, weaned on her pile of siblings. And we want to touch her back. We reach for her scruff, for the felty tips of her ears; we lay our hands on her warm belly and tickle our fingers on her neck under her collar.

She first became aware of her own tail when it grew long enough to curl over and touch her back, surprising her. Now I see her at times lying on her side watching her own tail wag and grabbing at it. Over the months it has grown more voluminous: a feathery curve dangerously on the move. Because I have a son who might take ten photos of the puppy in a second, I have evidence of precisely how her tail wags. Left to right, of course, but not just left, right. On each side, the final moment of wag has the white tip of her tail curling almost to touch her back, then slingshotting back to wag the other way. She will complete just two steps—right foot, left foot—during a cycle of her normal, merrily-walking-around-the-house wag. Her someone-is-definitely-at-the-door wag is almost twice as fast. Her it's-morning-oh-my-god-hello-I've-missed-you wag is impossible to capture on film, seeing as her entire body is a wiggling jelly.

As Quid's tail ramps up, Finnegan's tail has stopped wagging. He has been diagnosed with a degenerative disease that progressively paralyzes from the rear forward. His run is a hop, not unlike Quid's first attempts at running: the back legs operating together, the front body doing all the work. I see the frustration on his face as he cannot climb the stairs without assistance and is slow to attack Quid as she runs by. We are assured that, by definition, paralysis is not painful. But I mourn the loss of his tail wag and lament all the quiet pauses where a tail thump used to be. On my desk where I write, a photo of young Finnegan smiles at me, his tail midwag, as he heads straight for my camera. Now Quid will have to wag for two.

☕

Apart from our inability to fly, the absence of a tail in humans is, to me, our greatest evolutionary sorrow. Worse, we had tails at one point and now have only a vestigial tailbone, the coccyx. Human embryos of four weeks have a tail that curls toward their head; it is typically lost by nine weeks (although there are rare instances of babies born with a caudal appendage). The canid tail has up to twenty-three vertebrae—nearly as many as the rest of their spine. It is truly a multitasking limb, involved in movement, balance, communication, and expression of emotion. This is one reason why tail docking—literally cutting off much or nearly all the tail—is being banned in more countries, although not yet in the United States, where a docked tail is still part of many purebred dogs' breed standards, for antiquated reasons. Docking is painful, can lead to chronic pain, and results in loss of this hugely expressive and important limb.

Happily there is a small field of tail-wag science, which looks at the context and meaning of various tail postures and velocities. They tell us that six stages of tail height can be measured, from the highest (straight up from the base) to the third highest (straight back), then relaxing, going under the body, and curling around the body when lying on the ground. Tails are used differentially in everything from "upright trot" and "investigative approach" (highest) to fear (under the body) and sleep (around the body). What scientists call "lateral tail movements"—what everyone else calls tail wagging—add additional meaning. Far from just showing happiness, the rate of tail wagging changes in different contexts: part of happy greetings, as a threat, before mating, in play, when alarmed, when finishing stretching, and even waiting to be let outside.

Look even more closely, and the tail wag's message is more specific. When dogs see their person, or someone else they are eager to greet, their tail wag is more right wag than left wag; when they see an unknown dog, tail wagging veers left. Most of the body is mapped cross-laterally to the brain, so a left-wagging tail is connected to the right side of the brain—specializing in hesitation or withdrawal. The right-wagging tail connects to the left hemisphere, associated with approach behavior. Watching a dog's tail in slow motion gives a little peek into their mind.

Wags are sufficiently tuned to dogs' internal experience that researchers can count wags to determine how excited dogs are. Highly excited dogs might wag an average of 125 times in a minute, or 2 wag laps a second. (Quid's tail, sometimes zooming into a blur, is certainly above this average.)

Watch a bird dog track their bird and you will see a wag rate indicative of tremendous excitement. Though it has not been studied as closely as social interaction, the tail is surely a glimpse into what dogs experience through smell as well. They smell where you have been, who you have been with, and what other dog you have petted. Their tails, keeping a thoughtful tempo, tell us how they might feel about that dog you were tickling.

One of the greatest pleasures of the puppy is her willingness to be tickled, petted, and rubbed—her solicitation of contact. With the pandemic, social contact was cut off; dogs became proxies for other people in our homes and our outlet for literal connection. We might forget how it feels to sit close enough to someone that your legs are touching or you can smell their shampoo, but Quid naturally stretches out her body to achieve full contact with mine (and will allow my cozying up to her). That contact is a reminder of the pleasure of the simplest of human contact, too: the hug or slight touch from family and friends. Dogs could not have been more perfectly designed to scratch that itch.

Petting a dog is, in fact, healthy for us. It affects our immune system by increasing levels of the antibody immunoglobulin A, which is important to immune function, anxiety levels, blood pressure, and heart rate—you name it. The pleasurable rush from the touch of a loved one can be reproduced by reciprocating with a dog. The dog you pet need not even be your own, just a fur-covered, doe-eyed member of the species. There is a small subliterature asking if petting makes the dog feel better, too. Unfortunately, as with much mid-twentieth-century research, scientists tried to make their subjects feel bad first. When they shocked a dog's paws, then petted the dog, petting decreased the big spike in heart rate that the shock induced. *Bad researchers.* More-enlightened researchers find naturally distressing situations and simply see if they can make the dogs feel better about them. Army dogs and shelter dogs preferred petting to praise as a reward—sometimes more than food. What counts as petting varies in these studies: it is usually a variation on long firm strokes from head to rump. Less easy to characterize, for person and dog alike, is the affection that is conveyed from person to dog and back again via the petting hand. That's the magic bit.

JANUARY ❀ NEARLY 1 YEAR
Lick, Memory

It is one week shy of a year since the day Quiddity was born. I remember not knowing her, but my memories of her are already changed by the dog I know now. I wonder if we, in turn, have completely replaced the memory of her actual mother, of the constant company of her siblings.

Those first weeks of her life were full of such impulses and frustrations, noise and smell, body upon body. Now she hops neatly up on the sofa and orients herself toward me, watching me with surprising interest while I eat a pear. She has figured out, with very little help, how to be a dog among dogs and how to be a dog among people. Sometime in there she became herself.

And we became able to see her for who she is. It is hard to see, initially. In today's culture, puppies come to us, from breeder or shelter, with the reputation of their breed or parents already seeming to define who they are. So we all come to the experience of having a puppy with ideas about how it's going to go, who that puppy is going to be. We prepare with books that claim to inform us about how puppies behave—not unlike the user's guide for our new tablet. We think we're ready. We think they will be an easy addition to our lives. We think they will sleep through the night, will understand us, will want what we want. We're wrong, of course.

Worse, our expectations distract us from seeing the delicious new, difficult, and budding personality that is there.

With this in mind, I have made a new list of What You Need to Be Prepared for Your Puppy. Are you ready? Do you have somewhere you can write this down? A pen? Okay, then. Here is the list.

Requirements

1. Expect that your puppy will not be who you think, nor act as you hope.

That's it! That's the list.

Of course, I was glimpsing some of who she was when I first met her. The farther she is from her siblings, the more I see in Quid signs of her time among her blood relatives. The way she lies with us—her body tracing the length of my leg, her head resting on my lap, or sometimes all of her resting on my lap—simulates the time of her youth, huddled up next to, on top of, and under her siblings. It began as a way to keep warm; it became a sign of affection and affiliation. Alongside one another she and Upton dig their noses deep into each other's fur, evocative of that time before vision was on line—when other dogs were defined only by their smell and warmth, and to get more of both, you burrowed closer.

In quiet moments, when I peek over the top of my book and see her lying with her eyes open, gazing nowhere, I wonder if she is reminiscing about her young puppyhood. If she looks for her mother in the dog she spots approaching on the sidewalk or coming over the hill. If she thinks about the day she arrived home, on a leash for the first time, and huddled under our feet as the dogs probingly sniffed her. If she pines for her siblings.

One day, we find out. The sky is unnaturally blue, the air expectant. Over Quid's head we have talked about this day for weeks: two of her faraway siblings are coming to see her. She pads alongside me throughout the morning, lying down at my feet with a sigh when I sit at my desk—up until the moment two cars pull up the driveway.

She lifts her head, her ears satellite dishes tuned to the arrival. The first car quiets; a door opens. She barks, and the car barks back: it is Luna (I knew her as Persimmons as a puppy). I remember her being sweetly predisposed to lap sitting. As we greet them, I take her in: she is Quid-size, her coat merle gray, and she sports a splash of blue in one eye, giving her a look of constant alarm. She hops out of the car gracefully and noiselessly (as Quid does), then looks with uncertainty at her person holding her leash (as Quid does not). We start walking to the house, talking/barking as we go. The pups walk astride each other, both light on their toes, both loud of voice. They are aware of each other, to be sure, but do they recognize each other?

What would recognition look like? Well, Quid certainly recognizes us when we return home; she recognizes the cat; she recognizes canine friends. With us, recognition is visible in the speed with which an alarm bark morphs into a friendly warble, in the softening of her ears from erect and alert to pressed back against her head.

I look at her and Luna. Both wear a stiff-wagged, perked-eared pose, their barks pointed exclamation marks. While there is much resemblance between the two, I don't see any immediate signs of familiarity. Yet, over several minutes, they become comfortable with each other—considerably more quickly than usual with an unknown dog. It is as if they see themselves in each other—and soon become less concerned with this "strange dog" beside them.

Similarly when Coren—previously Cholla Cactus—joins the pair. He is 50 percent bigger than the two girls, with a natural smile. They all sport white tips to their tails and white-paint-dipped feet; feathering graces the backs of their legs. And, more strikingly, they are similar of style, with the same intent gaze, the same gazelle-like running and explosive energy. Yet he, too, shows no clear acknowledgment of these pups with whom he shared the first, formative weeks of life. They mill around one another, alternating play with exploration (Coren), entreaties to her owner (Luna), or fixation on getting a tennis ball tossed (Quid).

At one point, when I have ducked inside, I hear Quid's shrill, piercing bark. I peek out the window to see what she's announcing. What I see is Quid lying down, her eyes on a ball, her pose serene and focused. She makes not a sound. To my delight, it is the two others barking her bark. For once, our pup is not the loudest in the scene.

⇝

By the age of one year, young dogs are the equivalent of thirty-year-old adolescents: their bodies have mostly developed, but their brains (and their behavior) have not. The signs of raw youth have waned. Blue eyes have nearly all darkened, the pink pads of their feet have turned spotted and then have darkened with age. Bodies have grown into proportion with heads, faces with eyes. Yet they are still works in progress, just on the edge of familiarity with their place in our world.

This year, this dreadful year for the world, brought more dogs than ever into people's homes. In a survey by our lab of people who adopted dogs in the months after the pandemic became globally recognized in March 2020, a third had not been planning to add a dog to their family. Why now? "Everyone was home to help with the transition," one respondent said; another reflected many people's feelings of the desirability of having a dog when working from home. Among people filling out the survey, the experience was challenging ("Hardest thing I've ever done") but rewarding ("She has kept me sane"; "They've changed the lives of everyone in this house").

Nonetheless, the chance that some of these pups will wind up returned to a shelter or breeder, or even abandoned or electively euthanized, is not small. One busy animal shelter, the Charleston Animal Society in South Carolina, homed almost ten thousand dogs in four years (from 2015 to 2019) but saw more than fifteen hundred returned in that time—and that was prepandemic. The highest rates of return were of young adults around Quid's age: the adolescents who test boundaries and have grown out of their deep puppy cuteness. A third of them were returned because of the dog's behavior—especially their activity level, perceived aggression to people or other animals, and their destructive behavior. Exactly zero people said they returned their dog because the dog was "not friendly."

This shelter's experience jibes with another large-scale study, in which so-called behavioral problems were cited by 40 percent of people who gave up their dog. Our own puppy has been full of "behavioral problems." She is active, can bark rudely at people and animals, and continues to eat various nonedible, and sometimes valuable, items. But she is Quid. I am already starting to forget the long nights, the frustrations, the troubles.

For a year as full as the first year of life is, it is not obvious that a one-year-old puppy has much memory of it at all. They do know how and where and what. Researchers have confirmed that dogs have memories of specific events. One group trained their subjects to imitate a person's actions, whatever they did. Then the dogs were shown a brand-new action—like touching an open umbrella or walking around a bucket—and the dogs were asked to replicate it after a delay. Nearly all of them remembered the novel actions and could perform them themselves.

But the kind of memory we wonder about is, of course, the one we treasure ourselves: our own memories. I can think back to my fifth birthday, joined by friends and my family, eyeing a well-frosted cake on a picnic table. Do dogs remember their lives in this way? No research has confirmed that they do yet—not because dogs cannot, but because it is difficult to ask non-language-using subjects to recall something earlier in their past for you.

But studies hint strongly at the prospect that dogs do remember. And given how strongly linked to the past odors can be—and how central odors are to dogs' lives—one might imagine that some of these memories are encoded in smells. The preference puppies show for the smell of their siblings, and the ease with which they interact with those long-lost siblings when reunited, is suggestive. It is possible that their memories of their own past rush back just like ours do when they get a whiff of a familiar, long-ago scent.

By the age of one year, pups are part of the human family: they will turn to their people over their siblings; they know the habits, style, and treat-giving potential of each of their family members; they are attached. Even without either party consciously trying, the dog-person bond is forged. One day I look up at the face biting my nose and I find it delightful—something I've come to expect and await. She is no longer a stranger; she is ours, and we are hers.

🦴

On the morning of her birthday, Quid arrives on the bed as if cannon-shot and beelines for my face to lick my mouth. Then she circles around and delivers mouth licks to Finnegan, to Upton, to Ammon, and to Edsel, who has been unwise enough to follow Quid upstairs. Then she races downstairs and mouth-licks our son.

I know intellectually what she is doing. She is greeting us; she is showing her affection for us; she is trying to get our attention: all those things at once. Her manner is so completely efficient and thorough that as I lie there, hiding my face under the sheet against the second round, I get another idea of what she is doing. Each morning Quid faces what to her are a series of unresponsive, still bodies. Perhaps she believes that she is giving us life with her licks. Indeed, an exceptionally good lick brings a whole lot of life all of a sudden: we may rise straight out of bed, uttering a great sound. She knows best to back away then, to stand vigilant over this new life she has created—and definitely not to lick again.

This is like nothing more than what Maize did a year ago today, as she licked her puppies into life. On a walk with my family, as Quid checks in on everyone, nosing each of us in turn, I see her mother again, poking her nose into the pen holding eleven mewling eggplant-shaped pups to count that everyone is there.

And hasn't she given us life? Our family's story of the pandemic, like those of innumerable other families, includes sickness and loss and fear. But the story is also entangled with the chaos and joy brought by this complex furry character whom we have come to know. When the world kept its distance, she walked right up to the world and licked it in its face. She reminded us of—she embodied— the pleasure of life.

At the same time, I only later realized—after her energy became organized, after the pandemic released us from its grip—that it was her very vitality that had made it hard for me to love her. I was watching the vitality slip from Finnegan and inhabit Quid. Finn, who spent years running by my side—or sometimes running away, with a stolen ball in his mouth (sorry, Moose, for that ball we stole). Finn, whose tail wagged the most exuberant greetings; who leaped on the bed to find me under the covers; who rolled on his back with pleasure in the perfect dirt patch; who charged into puddles with his mouth wide and tail high. Finn was suddenly unable to run, to wag, to leap, to roll, to charge. I lamented his losses and felt his chagrin as he watched Quid seem to take his place. While he could move less each day, she could do every sort of move: neatly leap from a stand to the top of the dining table; launch herself into the air, mouth-first, after a high-bouncing ball; relax her shoulders to shimmy under the couch, back legs splayed. It was as though she had taken those movements from him, stolen them. I would not let her steal my love from him, too.

And she did not. Yet one day I find myself talking about "the dogs"—and meaning her to be among them. Slowly, reluctantly, over the year, two have become three. Somehow it has taken this long for us to realize that we didn't get *just* another dog. While there are plenty of resemblances between Quid, Finn, and Upton— they are all quadrupedal sniffers with kind faces, long tails, and a shared genetic history—we were really adding an entirely different person to the family. One who is not only a different age, but also a different personality, with a different set of skills, drives, concerns, sensitivities. And now, our family has one bearded lady.

I smile at that beard. At her eyebrows, her spectacular ears, at the *raoh-rooo!* she says to me in the morning. Our relationship bloomed despite my resistance. Dogs have, after all, evolved with us—may even have evolved us as a species. They sneak into our hearts because our hearts are tuned to their frequencies. Over the year I removed my scientific cap more often and just let her be.

Quid, in her being who she is and not who I hoped or imagined she would be, reminds me that it is less who I want our puppy to be than who I want to be with our puppy. I return from a trip and open the door, happy to see her. I invite her for naps and belly rubs; I put down my work to toss a tennis ball for her to go bananas over. I welcome her changeability, her enthusiasm. I look forward to what mercurial spirit will grab her next.

Do I love her?

How could I ever have not?

Good dog

Postscript

It's one year later: Quid has turned two. And we have just lost Finnegan and Upton, four weeks apart. Our family is suddenly changed, and a yawning hole is at its center.

The dogs filled every second of our days, and now their absence is felt in all those moments. It takes form in longing, in grief that they are gone, in melancholic remembrance. I miss Finn's winsome smile, formed of his panting mouth, soft eyes, and wagging tail. I miss Upton's howl at dinnertime, his akilter tail, and his gangly run. In the house, I miss sharing the space with them: hearing them shake when rising, their toenails on the floorboards, their cadence up the stairs, their breath and muffled noises in sleep. Outside, I miss following them on their explorations, feeling the invisible rubber band that joined us as we moved at our respective paces through a forest or park—Finn always circling back to us, Upton pulled farther by distant scents. I miss them galloping down the hall when I came home, circling around me and knocking my legs with their tails. I miss the way Finn would push his nose into my hand to guide me to pet his face and tickle his ear; I miss Upton's pawing of the air to ask us to continue rubbing the soft folded fur on his chest.

These dogs were worked into the fabric of our lives, into the sinews of our bodies. Quid lies on her back next to me now, head thrust backward, legs reaching to the ceiling, quiet. I stroke her ear aimlessly. These dogs.

Acknowledgments

Could I have written this book without you all? Quiddity, I literally could not have written it without you. But—and this holds extra true for Finnegan, Upton, and Edsel—what I moreover appreciate is your letting us keep your company.

And all the people around Quid! I want to thank Amy Hershberger, who fostered the litter—not only for her incredible generosity in taking in so many dogs being rehomed but also for entertaining my visits during those early weeks and into the pandemic. Thank you to Kara Gilmore, who runs the Hudson Valley Dog Farm, for connecting us with Amy and for her sage ideas. Thank you to the other families who adopted Maize and her puppies—Pumpkin (Romeo), Acorn, Blue Camas (Blü), Cranberry, Fiddlehead, Persimmons (Luna), Chaya, Flint, Pawpaw (Chutney), Cholla Cactus (Coco/Coren)—for glimpses of the parallel universes of these young sprites.

Seung Suh and Bob Caccamise—and Caine and Bullitt—you were essential parts of this year. Alison Curry and Layla, thank you for city picnics and treasured companionship; Gayle Edgerton and Jaxx, thanks for the pandemic walks. Susan and Georgie, sorry about the barking. Thank you to people whom I consulted along the way: Maggie Howell, Cheri Asa, Soon Hon Cheong; Roxanne Bok and Linda Seaver; Amy Attas and Karen Becker. Thank you to Jesse Freidin for photography tips, to Pat Goodman and Karen Davis at Wolf Park for wolf tips, and to those working at or with the WDC family: Jenny Essler, Dana Ebbecke, Amritha Mallikarjun, Cindy Otto, and Alice Barnhart. Thanks to Anna Lai at Muddy Paws and Mike Rose, foster to Viola and her pups and dad to Boots.

Thank you to my agent and friend, Kris Dahl, for boosting the good book ideas and gently stamping out the bad ones. Thanks to Wendy S. Walters, Betsy Carter, Aryn Kyle, Maira Kalman, Jennifer Vanderbes, Sally Koslow, and Elizabeth Kadetsky for regular writerly inspiration at our obligatory distance and to Maneesha Deckha and Daniel Hurewitz for keeping me honest—both to the story and to the schedule. Thank you to Brad Mehldau for unwittingly providing the soundtrack to many, many paragraphs.

To Ken Wright, Meriam Metoui, the many copy- and art editors who contributed their time and wisdom, and everyone at Viking Children's Books, thank you for welcoming this puppy. To Catherine Frank, thank you for your attention to our readers' point of view. The enthusiasm and ideas of you all have made this book what it is.

Thank you to my natal family, Damon and Elizabeth: every story comes from you originally. Most of all, Ammon and Ogden, thank you for reading drafts, entertaining sentences, and egging me on—and thank you for how you love Quiddity.

INDEX

Page numbers in *italics* indicate images.